Lesbian Motherhood in Europe

Edited by
KATE GRIFFIN
and LISA A. MULHOLLAND

CASSELL

London and Washington

For a catalogue of related titles in our Sexual Politics/Global Issues list please write to us at:

Cassell
Wellington House
125 Strand
London WC2R 0BB

PO Box 605
Herndon VA 20172

First published 1997

British Library Cataloguing-in-Publication Data
A catalogue record for this book is available from the British Library.

ISBN 0 304 33311 5 (hb)
     0 304 33312 3 (pb)

Designed by Geoff Green

Printed and bound in Great Britain by Biddles Ltd,
Guildford and King's Lynn

Other titles in Cassell's 'Queer Families' series include:

Challenging Conceptions: Planning a Family by Self-Insemination
LISA SAFFRON

We Are Family: Testimonies of Lesbian and Gay Parents
TURAN ALI

What About the Children? Sons and Daughters of Lesbian and Gay Parents Talk About Their Lives
LISA SAFFRON

There Must Be 50 Ways to Tell Your Mother: Coming-Out Stories
LYNN SUTCLIFFE

Sister and Brother: Lesbians and Gay Men Talk About Their Lives Together
Edited by JOAN NESTLE and JOHN PRESTON

Contents

Acknowledgements

We would like to thank all the women who agreed to be interviewed for this book, and who took the time to fill out and return the questionnaires. We would also like to thank our profile writers for researching and compiling information and for organizing interviews and circulating questionnaires. Thanks must also go to the following organizations for providing information: CIRCA Research and Reference Information Ltd., Cambridge; Homodok, Amsterdam; ILGA, Brussels; EuroLetter, Copenhagen.

Lisa would like to thank, in no particular order, the following people: Dana Sa'd and Aimée Schimmel for their proofreading and encouragement throughout the writing process. Petra Jedlicková and Dáša Frančiková of the Prague Gender Studies Center for their help compiling materials and sources. Lenka Králová for translation, sources and doing the dishes even when it wasn't her turn. Helen (Grandma) Mulholland for sharing her new computer over the Christmas holidays, 1995. The staff of the Prague Post Foundation for sharing space with the project and putting up with deadline stress. Jana Štěpánová for sources, interviews and general helpfulness. The staff of *Promluv* magazine and organization for their publication and lesbian events. Petra Teuschel and the staff of the Elektra e-mail server of the Woman Frauen-Mailbox-Netzwerk in Heidelberg, Germany, for providing free e-mail service and the loan of computer equipment. Uli Streib for book consultation during the summer of 1995. ILIS in Amsterdam for their important international lesbian newsletter. Frauen Anstiftung e.V. for supporting projects to get women organized, on-line and accessible. Long Live Hippo Camp!

Kate would like to thank Liz and Peter Griffin, for their long-distance encouragement. Milou De Dobbeleer, for support and childcare, and Audrey Van Tuyckom, for translation and helping out at the last minute. Masha Gessen, for reading and rereading and offering constructive criticism and insights, and for stimulating me at every level. Alba Griffin, for patiently believing that her mother would one day finish this book.

Contributors

SHELLEY ANDERSON is a freelance editor and journalist living in the Netherlands. She volunteers with the International Lesbian Information Service, for whom she wrote *Lesbian Rights are Human Rights*! She doesn't have any children, but she is a very popular aunt and grandmother.

CECILIA BERGGREN is 39, and has been involved in RFSL for many years both at local and national levels. She was previously the vice-president of RFSL, and now works as secretary of the RFSL federation.

JENNIFER BROWN was born in Whitefish, Montana. She studied and taught in Szeged, Hungary from 1991 to 1993 and has travelled extensively in Central Europe and the Balkans. She finnished her MA in journalism at the American University in Washington DC in 1994 and returned to Hungary to work. Besides covering Hungary and the Balkans for general and trade publications, she edits the Internet newsletter *The Hungary Report*.

PERE CRUELLS is a lectura in mathematics at the Universitat Poitecnica de Catalunya. He is a volunteer at the Commission for International Affairs of the Coordinadora Gai-Lesbiana (CGL), working on ILGA issues, and at the Commission for Gay and Lesbian Rights of the CGL.

DANIELA DANA was born in Milan in 1967. She has worked as a journalist for the gay magazine *Babilonia*. In 1994 she published *Amiche, Compagne Amanti: Storia Dell 'Amore Tra Donne*, a history of love between women, the first major book on the subject to appear in Italy. She is now working on a book about the legal recognition of homosexual couples.

MICHELE DE DOBBELEER is the mother of two teenage daughters.

CATHERINE DONOVAN is a researcher at the University of Sunderland.

DÁŠA FRANČIKOVÁ has worked at the Gender Studies Centre since 1995. She is a volunteer with Amnesty International and is following studies on Women's Human Rights and Gay/Lesbian Human Rights.

BARBARA FRÖLICH is an activist with HOSI Vienna

MASHA GESSEN is a Moscow-based journalist, writing for publications in Russia, the US and the UK. She is the author of *Rights of Lesbians and Gay Men in the Russian Federation: An International Gay and Lesbian Human Rights Commission Report* (San Francisco, 1994)

KATE GRIFFIN lives in Moscow and works as an editor for Russian and British news organizations. She has a daughter, Alba.

RUTH HOWALD is Swiss, 32 years old, born in Germany. She lived in the US for two years from 1990-92, as a social work intern. She has worked as a music teacher in state schools, but now she is a physiotherapy student. She was on the board of LOS from 1994-96 and served as president. She has given interviews on television, radio and in newspapers on lesbian rights, and has conducted workshops for social work students.

LILLIAN KOTTER is one of the founders of the Estonian Lesbian Union.

PAULA KUOSMANEN is doing research on lesbian motherhood. Her topic is 'Lesbian Motherhood in Modern Gender Systems in Finland'. She has lectured and written articles on lesbian motherhood. In the 1980s she worked as an active feminist in Helsinki and in the 1990s she turned to genderblending lesbian activists. Lately she has concentrated on research.

THOMAS E. LAVELL III was associated with *Lambda Warszawa* and was working as the English editor at the *Warsaw Voice* in Poland at the time he compiled the report. He has since moved to Vienna.

GRO LINSTAD was born in 1960. She lives in Oslo with her life partner Bente. Since 1993 she has been president of the Norwegian national organization for Lesbian and Gay Liberation.

LISA MULHOLLAND is the director of a not-for-profit organization in Prague. She teaches gender studies via English language courses and writes on sexuality and gender issues.

KATI MUSTOLA teaches lesbian studies at the University of Helsinki and is researching lesbian and gay history in Finland. 'I was straight and married until thirty-something, but had no children at that time. I got my first child (a daughter of four years) with my first lesbian relationship. That is how I became a lesbian co-mother; or a lesbian father, as I sometimes provocatively call myself. Three years later I became mother (or father) a second time, this time of a son, at whose birth I was present.'

VIBEKE NISSEN is a practising psychologist with an MA in psychology. She is co-founder and former headmistress of 'Kvindehøskolen' (Feminist School). She has been active from the start in the women's and lesbian movements, including international networking and organization. She has been a member of ILGA (International Lesbian and Gay Association) Women's Secretariat and was a research librarian at KVINFO, Centre for Interdisciplinary Information on Women's Studies. She works professionally with battered women and terminally ill patients (cancer and AIDS).

INGE-LISA PAULSEN is editor of PAN-*Bladet*, the membership magazine of LBL, the Danish national organization for gays and lesbians. She is a translator, writer and publisher, with an MA in English and Drama, and has done post-graduate work in England and the USA. She holds teaching and research positions in Danish universities, and is active in ILGA (International Lesbian and Gay Association).

ADELAIDE PENHA E COSTA is involved in the lesbian organization Lilas. She studied art in Lisbon and Brussels and works as an illustrator and painter.

IRENE PETROPOULOU is a freelance translator of technical and scientific articles. 'I got mixed up with the gay and lesbian movement in 1982 for the first time. Until 1987 I worked with lesbian groups and later with AKOE (The Greek Homosexual Liberation Movement), and later with EOK (Greek Homosexual Community). I am one of the persons that formed this community in 1988.

My work now has to do with activities of the community, with the Women's Caucus of EOK, with writing articles about lesbianism (sometimes) and with preparing once a month a one-hour program about lesbians.'

PATRICIA PRENDIVILLE works for a community development support and training organization called *Meitheal*, which is based in Dublin. Her work includes facilitation, training, consultancy and research. Publications include *Sugar and Spice: A Resource Book for Working with Young Women*, (NYCI, Dublin, 1993), *Developing Facilitation Skills: A Handbook for Facilitators*, (CPA, Dublin 1995) and *Poverty, Lesbians and Gay Men: The Economic and Social Effects of Discrimination* (GLEN and CPA,

Dublin, 1995). She is involved in a number of women's groups, and has been active in women's movement activities in Ireland since returning to Dublin in 1987.

ALENKA PUHAR is a journalist and psychohistorian who lives and works in Ljubljana, Slovenia.

MAUREEN SHARP is a correspondent in Vilnius for the English language newspaper *Baltic Observer*.

CLAIRE TIJSBAERT is a counsellor and group facilitator who works with lesbian women and couples. She lives with her partner and their three year-old daughter, and has two grown-up sons.

AUDREY VAN TUYCKOM is a freelance translator working in English and Dutch.

MONIKA WIENBECK was born in 1963 and grew up in West Germany; she has lived in West Berlin since 1985. She has made regular visits to the GDR since 1972. Her studies include philosophy, linguistics, German literature, politics and jurisprudence. Her political development began with the peace movement. She then became involved in grassroots and feminist students' groups, the pro-choice movement, a women's self-defence club. Coming-out as a lesbian in 1991, she has been seriously active in the political lesbian scene since 1994.

NICOLA WILLIAMS is a correspondent in Riga for the English-language newspaper *Baltic Observer*.

HANNAH WOLFSON is a staff writer with the English-language newspaper *The Slovak Spectator* in Bratislava, Slovakia.

ANTONIA YOUNG is a Research Associate in Sociology/Anthropology, Colgate University, USA and Honouary Research Fellow at the Research Unit in South East European Studies, Bradford University, UK. She has focused her study on the Balkans over three decades, and has spent time in Albania every year since 1989. Co-editor of *Black Lambs and Grey Falcons: Women Travellers in the Balkans* (Bradford University, 1991), she has also written on gender issues in the Balkans.

Kate's Story

The inspiration for this book struck at three o'clock in the morning, 31 January 1994 as I was writing the covering letter for my entry to the Cassell Award for Lesbian Non-Fiction Writing. I had seen this competition advertised in the UK's national lesbian and gay newspaper the Pink Paper, calling on lesbians to write a short article on any issue of interest to the lesbian community, and had decided to write on a subject I knew through personal experience – lesbian motherhood.

My six-year-old daughter Alba and I had been living in Brussels for just over two years, during which time I had felt particularly isolated. Most of the lesbians I knew didn't have children, the few lesbian mothers I had met all had grown-up children, and I found I had little in common with the heterosexual mothers at Alba's school. In comparison, the UK sounded like paradise, if the articles I read in the Pink Paper were anything to go by. A lesbian baby boom! Lesbian mother support networks! Even my mother was starting to clip articles from the mainstream newpapers to send to me.

But what was the story in the rest of Europe? A few days previously I had received a letter from my friend Jana at the Czech lesbian magazine Promluv, asking me to write an article on my own experience as a lesbian mother. I realized then that discussion about parenting by lesbians was more than just a UK phenomenon, and I was curious to know more.

I didn't win the competition, but Cassell liked my suggestion for a book exploring the different experiences of lesbian mothers across Europe. Alba and I liked the idea too. I wanted to meet women from other countries and swap stories, while Alba wanted to meet children from families where having a lesbian mother was normal, no big deal.

When Cassell commissioned the book from me, I soon realized that to gather information about lesbian mothers from all across Europe was no small undertaking, and maybe I needed help … enter Lisa, an American friend living in Prague. We decided to share out the work: from my Brussels location I took responsibility mostly for the countries of western Europe, while Lisa focused more on the east.

Knowing where to begin was difficult, but once I started making contacts the process took on a momentum of its own. First I concentrated on finding lesbian researchers from each country to write the profiles, writing seemingly hundreds of letters and e-mail messages to friends, friends of friends, women I'd met once at conferences, national lesbian and gay organizations and publications. After a while the ball started to roll, and my contact in one country would recommend a friend of hers in another. Finding profile writers in countries with a well-established lesbian and gay infrastructure such as the Netherlands, Denmark, Norway and Sweden was quite straightforward, but the countries of southern Europe proved more problematic. My letters to Spain went unanswered, my letters to Greece were returned. In the end the answer turned out to be e-mail, as lesbian organizations in those two countries came on line and I started getting replies. By this time, late 1995, I had moved to Russia to live with my lover Masha, and almost all my communication with the outside world was via the Internet.

From September 1994 until February 1996 I interviewed lesbian mothers in the UK, Belgium, Russia and any other country to which I had the opportunity to travel through my work for a European women's organisation. Only on three occasions were Lisa and I able to carry out an interview together, the rest we conducted individually. On one occassion in Poland, I was introduced to Joanna, the only out lesbian mother in that country; she agreed to be interviewed at her home, with a friend acting as interpreter. The following year I was sitting in a Warsaw street cafe with Masha when Joanna walked past, struggling to push her pram over the uneven pavement. She recognized Masha straight away, as they're old friends, but I was amused to see that she had no idea who I was – giving an interview to some foreigner about lesbians in Poland was clearly so frequent an occurrence that it made little impression on her.

Another time Lisa, Alba and I went on a daytrip to the Netherlands to meet Clare and Debbie, two friends of mine from the UK, who were staying in Amsterdam for a week. The children went out for a walk to the park with their grandmother, leaving us with a few rare moments of peace to take a rest from living our hectic lives as lesbian mothers, and to talk about it instead.

During a business trip to Italy, Alba and I spent a very pleasant Sunday afternoon as guests of Bianca and Loretta. (I interviewed Bianca in the kitchen, while Loretta and Alba watched Mary Poppins dubbed into Italian in the other room). By coincidence we were in Italy at the same time as the lesbian film festival, so once my meetings were over, Alba and I hopped on the train to Bologna. Standing outside a building that we and several other women mistakenly thought was a venue, I struck up a conversation with Christina and her lover Patrizia. As it turned out, Alba was not the only child at the film festival, but Christina had left her son with friends, as boys were not allowed. Alba, by now rather bored with films dubbed into Italian, even if they were about lesbians, was happy to spend time with a child her own age. Our trip ended on Alba's birthday with a big breakfast celebration at Patrizia's, followed by the inevitable interview in Patrizia's tiny office while the kids sat watching the inevitable film dubbed into Italian.

As it was not possible to visit all the countries in Europe to carry out interviews in person, Lisa and I decided to use the interview questions to draw up a questionnaire, copies of which we sent to our profile writers to circulate. The biggest response came from Denmark, as the questionnaire was distributed among the members of a lesbian parenting group, who filled it in themselves and then passed it on to all their friends.

Adverts placed in lesbian and gay publications for lesbian mothers willing to fill in the questionnaire led to another interview, this time in my own home. After a couple of mysterious phone calls from a closeted French lesbian couple living on the outskirts of Brussels, we arranged to meet for tea at my place one Sunday afternoon. They had moved to Brussels from France with their daughter about a year previously, but had found it difficult to make friends in the lesbian scene – all loud music and drinking, no chance to talk. When they spotted my advertisement, it seemed like an ideal opportunity to meet other lesbian mothers, to start to break out of their isolation. As a result of our meeting I introduced them to my ex-girlfriend, who has two daughters. But just as it seemed that I might realize my desire to set up some kind of support network for lesbian mothers in Brussels, I met the woman of my dreams and moved to Russia to live with her.

A new country, new language and new school was not Alba's dream come true, however, and she decided to move back to the UK to live with her father, his girlfriend and her two sisters, visiting me and Masha during the school holidays. It was not, and still is not, an easy transition, from having a very close relationship with Alba, to seeing her for only two months a year. We miss each other very much, as financial considerations limit the amount of times we can visit, and regular phone conversations and e-mail messages do not compensate for this. Alba came over to Russia for her first visit in December 1995, and discovered that it wasn't so bad after all. It had its good points – snow, dogs and the ballet. Her relationship with Masha also moved on from when they first met in May – screams of 'it's my mother!' with all the rage and frustration of a jealous seven-year-old. One evening over dinner Masha was telling Alba about her dark-haired mother's dream of having blonde children. 'Well, now you have a blonde daughter' was Alba's reply.

My move to Russia not only turned my personal life upside down but also had a profound influence on my work on this book. Communication with the outside world is not easy from this ninth-floor Moscow apartment. The postal system is a little unreliable, faxes are more often than not illegible, outside phone lines for non-Moscow calls are elusive – e-mail is the answer, but only when the system is up and accessible. My communication with Lisa had always been via e-mail, but now my search for profile writers was also limited to cyberspace. Having contacted most of the lesbians on line in Finland, I came across Kati, who not only provided information for the Finnish profile but also conducted a cyberspace interview based on our questionnaire. It took her six hours to write, and at the end I felt I knew her as well as any of the other lesbian mothers I had interviewed in person.

One of the major disadvantages of being a foreign lesbian/homosexual alien in Russia is that I cannot marry my lover and settle permanently; instead the visa regime is such that I have to leave the country every three months. During one of these trips I took the overnight train to Tallinn, and spent my time productively at the Estonian

Lesbian Union interviewing a lesbian mother, Lilian, with interpretation by Estonian profile writer Lilian Kotter.

Back in Russia, it is interesting to note that many of the lesbians I know are mothers, as most Russian women have children, with or without a husband or boyfriend. Lesbian mothers have started meeting on a regular basis at Triangle, the local lesbian and gay organization in Moscow, which is where I met Lena, the last woman I interviewed.

Now the research for this book is almost over, I have met lesbian mothers from one end of Europe to the other, Alba has made new friends and added another parent to her collection ... What next? More babies, maybe?

Moscow, April 1996

Lisa's Story

When Kate asked me if I would become the eastern/central European co-editor of a book called *Lesbian Motherhood in Europe* I agreed quickly before she had an opportunity to withdraw the offer. After all, trying out the key words 'lesbian', 'mother' and 'Europe', I only score 33 per cent, being neither a mother nor European.

Those (small) points aside, I have lived in Prague, for almost six years, with a sixteen-month break to study for an MA in 'Women and Development' in The Hague. Since childhood I have been fascinated by children and hope to have at least two living in my household at some point in the near future. Being with children professionally as counsellor and teacher as well as friend, I have been accorded the title 'Aunty' in five languages and feel enlivened by close friendships I have developed with several young people.

My motivation for writing this book is partly a search for my own future and partly a continuation of a more academic line. As one of the educated white Americans who poured into (the then) Czechoslovakia, I have watched with fascination the interaction between Western ideals of feminism and lesbian activism and the various institutions and individuals in eastern Europe. Co-editing this book has provided the opportunity to gather information from all corners of Europe, establishing a feel for the vast differences which divide lesbian mothers as well as the basic things which link them together.

My first glimpse into lesbian motherhood occurred in 1988 during a summer camp session organized by the women living at the Twin Oaks community in rural Virginia, USA. At that time, children at Twin Oaks were being raised communally and a number of the primary parents were lesbians. When the occasion arose to write a paper for a class on redefining the American family I pulled on my boots and headed for the countryside. The issue of children in the community was being re-evaluated, and with the support of my summer camp friends I was welcomed and given plenty of information in the form of opinions and interviews. After graduating in 1990, I headed for Czechoslovakia and, while teaching English in a secondary school, began writing about the country's lesbian and gay population. I began to focus more specifically on eastern European lesbians and their families in 1994 for this book.

Without the use of information technology this project would have been a lot longer in the making, if not entirely impossible. Kate and I sent out requests for co-operation over various bulletin boards and pursued both profiles and interviews in cyberspace. Perhaps most importantly we communicated with each other, first between Brussels and Prague, then Prague and Moscow, over winter holidays between Moscow and Arizona and again Prague and Moscow: all via e-mail connections, made possible by Glasnet in Moscow and Elektra, a women-only BBS in Heidelberg, Germany.

Searching for information in eastern/central Europe I first tried, reasonably enough I thought, to find lesbian mothers to compile reports about their own countries. It soon became clear, however, that my logic was flawed, as very few of the mothers I contacted had the interest, ability, time and/or energy for such an undertaking. Linguistic differences proved a significant barrier and some women were uncomfortable with going out and publicly searching for facts and figures, thereby bringing attention to themselves and raising questions about their own sexuality.

Out of necessity I soon widened my pool of prospective profile writers, sending over one hundred and fifty letters by snail mail and e-mail to lesbian and women's groups,women journalists from those countries working in Prague and women on various mailing and conference lists. Made nervous by an initially poor reponse, I also wrote to embassies in Prague, England and the USA on behalf of the foundation for which I worked, requesting information under the cover of an enquiry about the status of women, families, the non-profit sector and, by the way, homosexuals. From thirty-six polite enquiries I received four answers – from the embassies of Slovenia, Latvia and Lithuania in Prague and the national office of statistics in Macedonia.

Next on the list were journalists from English-language publications in eastern/central European countries, which brought in several profiles, including the Polish one. I had contacted a 'women's issues' journalist at a newspaper in Warsaw and she promised to help. A few days later Tom Lavell called to clarify a few questions and to ask where he should fax the final product. Never having imagined that we would have a male writer, I hesitated a moment, then, overcoming my prejudice, gave him the information that he needed. Luckily for us, Tom turned out to be very knowledgeable. His profile is well prepared and we are grateful to have it.

On other occassions I would chase down anyone who seemed as if they might be remotely knowledgeable. This was the case with the Albanian profile. Half listening to the BBC World Service one day at work, I heard a story about what I thought were 'Swan Virgins' from a PhD student at 'Bradley' University. Three months later I had tracked down the writer – Antonia Young of Bradford University, UK, on loan to Colgate University, Hamilton USA. Antonia has extensively researched 'Sworn Virgins', women who take on prescribed male social roles in families living in the Albanian mountains. Contacted by e-mail, she was commissioned to write about Albania.

Interviews which I undertook personally or with a translator were mainly limited to the Czech Republic. A number of women welcomed me into their homes, but were quite reticent at first, uncomfortable with defining themselves as lesbian mothers. Some pointed out that they were bisexual because they had had sex to conceive the children or didn't mind sex with men. After a few questions, however, it was a fight to keep them on track as each of my queries was met with the mirror question, 'and what do other lesbian mothers say about it?'

Living in Prague, I was also able to use local lesbian events to meet lesbian mothers. One such event was a weekend in the countryside, where lesbian mothers and their children were warmly welcomed. At one point I found myself travelling back from a rock-climbing outing in an antique Skoda car with four lesbians who were mothers. After hearing about their children, they asked about mine. There was a moment of tension as I fumbled with the Czech language announcing that 'I no longer have a child'. A sigh of relief rushed through the strained silence as I realized my mistake and corrected myself, 'I mean, I don't have one yet.'

Prague, April 1996

Part One

Overview

1

Getting Kids
LISA A. MULHOLLAND

By definition, one of the great things about being a lesbian is not having to hold your breath waiting for your period after every sexual encounter. Yet what do you do when you *want* to 'get caught'? Bringing home baby is the end of one process and the beginning of another for all mothers, but lesbians are often forced to put more thought into both conceiving and raising that child than other parents. Pushing at social, political and religious boundaries, lesbian mothers in Europe are becoming more open than ever before about their lives and families, and women from all across the continent chose to contribute their personal stories and views to this book.

Greater visibility makes information about choosing motherhood and the options available more accessible. Artificial and self-insemination (AI and SI) are becoming well established as alternatives to more traditional methods. As in the past, women who have discovered their true sexuality are getting divorced from their husbands while maintaining custody of the children. Other methods of becoming a lesbian mother are still in use, as women have sexual intercourse with male friends and donors, while at the same time both lesbians and gay men are testing government boundaries over adoption and fostering.

In 1982 Monyek (a Dutch lesbian currently in her forties) and her former lover decided to have a child. They were one of the first couples in their Amsterdam community to do so and had few sources of information or role models to look to for help or advice. 'I always wanted children' explained Monyek, 'but I always put that away somewhere. Then I got to my thirtieth birthday. It wasn't usual then for lesbian women to think about having children but we thought "Well, we'll have to get one somewhere".'

Nowadays speaking openly about her family situation is not unusual for Monyek, an activist who works as a policy maker on an AIDS advisory committee. She has become a role model for other lesbians by going to court with her ex-lover, not to fight about the child but to try to get the non-biological parent's rights recognized. She currently lives in Amsterdam with her new lover and her thirteen-year-old son Koen. He divides his time between Monyek and her ex-lover, who lives down the street in the same complex of flats.

When Monyek and her former lover decided to become mothers they did not give much thought to AI. Monyek believes that this might have have been the next course of action had finding the right man been a problem. It wasn't, and she began to talk to an old friend and one time lover whom she trusted. A few months later he volunteered to be a donor, making it clear that although he did not want to be an active parent, he was willing to help Monyek and her partner. The first attempt at sexual intercourse was not successful, and Monyek and the donor both agreed that they would find it too difficult to continue. (Monyek's lover was also having problems accepting the process.) During the second attempt the friend ejaculated into a jar, after which Monyek's lover took over the inseminating activities. Luckily she became pregnant.

Monyek wanted, and was able, to get pregnant her own way, in her own home, mixing both contact with a donor and having her lover involved. Exploring other ways to be a birth mother, a lesbian who decides to try to become pregnant with the help of fertility clinics may find that she is refused service or placed on the bottom of a long waiting list. The ethics of fertility services continue to be discussed in academic and legal circles all over the world. Sometimes the debate spills over into public discussion when politicians make laws or via such sensationalized stories in the media as multiple births, women who conceive after menopause and so-called virgin-births (when a woman has a child without ever having heterosexual intercourse). The question of rights to insemination is a complex one. It seems to be accepted by the majority of the population Europe-wide that fertility clinics, where they exist, are primarily designed to assist married heterosexual couples. Single women and lesbians seeking artificial insemination are outside the main policy plan and are generally treated at best as if they had wandered into the wrong office and at worst as mentally ill.

In countries as diverse as Ireland, Slovenia, Portugal and Albania there is no prevailing law with regard to lesbians and artificial insemination. This is probably tied to several factors: first the procedures are not easily available, if they are practised at all; second, according to reports from these countries, there have been no organized efforts to obtain rights to AI; and third, there has been little media interest in the topic to date. Even those countries with a more developed AI infrastructure still may not have regulatory laws and typically leave the final decisions to the clinic administrator or individual doctors. For example, in Lithuania the cost of the procedure limits the number of AI providers to one – Dr Valentinas Matulevicius of Kaunas. He is able to choose his patients, and reports that he has treated only married couples. To his knowledge he has never assisted a lesbian to become pregnant and would refuse to do so if asked.

In Italy, following public outcry against lesbian insemination whipped up by media sensationalism, a law has been proposed to restrict the use of AI to heterosexual couples, ostensibly to ensure a child's right to a father. Like their colleague in Lithuania, Italian doctors involved in AI make their own decisions about whom they will treat. Unlike Dr Matulevicius, however, at least one Italian medical professional has assisted lesbian couples. When a Dr Ambrassa, speaking to a newspaper journalist in 1994, revealed that he had a lesbian couple among his patients, he was promptly suspended from CECOS (a professional organization for gynaecologists in the field of reproductive technology) for his efforts.

Denmark, Switzerland, Norway and Belgium have no laws restricting AI to heterosexual couples and leave the decision to health-care providers. Most insemination services are expensive, and not all women can afford them. Danish lesbians can and do use AI, normally with known donors, and lesbians from other countries can also travel to Denmark for treatment. While laws in Sweden directly prohibit AI through the health care system for those who are not in a heterosexual marriage, the rules in the Netherlands and the UK, albeit more complicated, may still have the same results.

In the Netherlands a proposed law will require previously anonymous donors to register, allowing children to learn the identity of their fathers if they later wish to do so. Not surprisingly, donations to sperm banks have decreased dramatically and in 1994 an AI provider in

Amsterdam announced that due to the shortage lesbians would be placed at the bottom of the waiting list. In the UK, the 1990 Human Fertilization and Embryology Act makes licensed clinics legally responsible for taking into account the welfare of the children who will result from their activities. This includes 'a child's need for a father'. The same Act also restricts the handling of any donated reproductive materials like sperm or ova to licensed professionals, thereby making SI or insemination with the help of a friend, while not directly illegal, fall outside of the law. To avoid the cost and difficulty of AI and seeing few other acceptable possibilities, some lesbians are willing to risk future legal difficulties such as custody battles and turn to SI, asking male friends to donate sperm or finding anonymous donors via friends.

In some countries known donors are still considered legal parents if the child in question was not the result of medically assisted AI. Self-inseminating mothers who later wish to receive state-sponsored childcare payments or other public assistance may run into trouble in Sweden, for example, if they are unwilling or unable to state the name of their child's biological or legal father. This has already happened in the UK, where women face a reduction of up to 20 per cent in certain forms of public assistance for refusing to disclose this information.

Women in Russia, on the other hand, are not restricted from receiving state support if they refuse to name the biological fathers of their children, no matter what form conception takes. After the birth of a child either the mother or father can take the documentation from the hospital and register the infant at the local registry office. Every registration must include the mother's name, but the 'father space' can be filled with the mother's husband's name, the name of a consenting male or left blank. Lesbian mothers can take advantage of this last option to protect themselves from any future custody claims or other problems. In addition, single mothers – that is women who were unmarried at the time of the birth, and where no father is indicated – receive additional state benefits.

Lena has three children: two boys aged thirteen and seven, and a nine-year-old girl. Her lover has one son, also nine years old. Lena has never been married, yet always knew she would have children. She had her children, 'before *perestroika*', as she puts it, when she was living as a lesbian in a heterosexual world: i.e. she had no lesbian friends and was dating straight women. Lacking information about alternative methods, she felt she had no other option but heterosexual intercourse. 'I entered sexual relations with men only with that goal,' she states wryly. She is officially a single mother and was careful not to list any fathers on her children's birth certificates. The older son has no contact with his father, but the father of the two younger children is welcome in Lena's home whenever he has time.

AI and SI provide simple opportunities to keep the biological father out of the lesbian family picture. AI draws its anonymous donors from sperm banks, and lesbians interested in SI have been known to enlist the aid of friends to work as go-betweens with one or more donor to assure confidentiality. Information about SI has not been widely available in Russia or other central and eastern European countries in the past. Interest is growing and more facts are being circulated in small lesbian magazines or via publications from other European countries. However, lacking the necessary details until only very recently, many central and eastern European lesbians have carried on getting children the 'old-fashioned way'. As the examples of Lena and Monyek illustrate, it is possible to have sexual relations with men for the sole purpose of creating a child, but what happens when a sexual partner doesn't realize that he is, in fact, a donor?

Sleeping with male friends and not telling them about their part in a resulting pregnancy, or setting up one-night-stands are also ways of getting pregnant without involving the donor in a father role. The latter method has some inherent difficulties. Health risks for both mother and child are significant. Unprotected sex with a stranger or casual acquaintance brings the threat of AIDS and/or other sexually transmitted diseases.

Sometimes the risks are considered worth it or not considered at all. Petra is an energetic and friendly woman in her mid-twenties who lives in a small flat in the suburbs of Prague with her lover Jana and their two children. Petra has a daughter named Klarka, a shy, cautious two-year-old with her mother's blue eyes and Jana has Hanka, a curious dark-haired adventurer who is three. Five years into their relationship Petra and Jana decided that they would each have a child. They were determined to get pregnant at the same time and were initially successful, but Petra had a miscarriage and had to begin again. Looking back on the situation Petra comments that having two babies at the same time would have been tremendously difficult as well as expensive.

Recalling the time four years before when she decided to get pregnant, Jana explains that she and Petra knew about AI but were sure no one in a hospital would assist them. Unaware of the procedure for SI they decided simply to get pregnant with men they knew without telling them. This plan has had complicated results. Currently Hanka sees her father about once a month as a family friend, but neither he nor the child are aware of their relation to one another. Klarka's father now knows she is his daughter and they spend one weekend a month together. He remains, however, unaware of Petra's sexual orientation. Petra reveals that she sleeps with him occasionally to ensure that he doesn't find out and create problems. She admits that it is probably only a matter of time before he makes the discovery.

Petra does not know any other lesbian mothers who conceived children in an established lesbian relationship rather than already having them from a heterosexual marriage. She is concerned about many aspects of lesbian child-raising and had as many questions for the interviewer as the interviewer had for her. She wanted to know what other women tell the biological fathers of their children and how much to tell the children themselves.

Jana and Petra took the path that seemed best for them at the time. They find now that it is a bit more complicated than they expected, but they have the children they so dearly desired. If they had tried to adopt or foster, they would probably still be waiting. The Czech Republic does not have any laws forbidding lesbian adoption, but those in charge of the already difficult process have voiced their objection to it during informal discussion and vowed to block known lesbians from adopting.

Lesbian experiences of fostering and adopting children who are not blood relatives (for example, nieces or nephews) are fairly similar across Europe. In many places out-lesbians have not yet tested their local laws and none of the countries for which we have information allow out-lesbians to adopt. A number of countries restrict adoption to married couples or at least prefer them to single-mother adoptions (the only way many lesbians may be successful).

The lack of access to adoption is a problem that is especially acute for lesbian couples who want to give the non-biological relationship to their child or children a legal basis. The nearest approximation in Europe to equal rights for the non-biological mother is the UK Residency Order introduced by the 1989 Children Act. This allows a person who resides with a child to apply for parental rights over that child. Although the law was originally intended to give rights to, say, grandparents raising their grandchildren, it does not specify that the person applying for the residency order has to be biologically related to the child, simply that they should be a "significant adult" in the child's life. At least three lesbian couples in the UK have already been successful in obtaining joint residence orders for both biological and non-biological mothers. As well as granting parental rights to the non-biological mother, the residency order also provides a legal basis for agreeing access rights in the case of separation, another situation in which the rights of the non-biological mother are not generally recognized. The main factor preventing lesbian couples in a similar situation from applying are the high court costs involved.

It is possible in most countries to make numerous other provisions, such as wills, legal statements detailing the biological mother's preference for custody in the event of her death, or pre-birth agreements to cover later partnership break-ups, but in the end these can be overruled by various court proceedings, especially if challenged by blood relatives of the surviving children. If biological mothers in the Netherlands make the request, lesbian co-parents (*meemoeders*) can be given some rights of supervision, for instance in a child's financial affairs, but even the *meemoeder* is not regarded as equal to the biological mother under Dutch law. The rules for fostering in many European countries are a bit more relaxed. In many cases decisions are left up to local councils, and children are placed with single women. Occasionally – as in a few recorded cases in Denmark, the Netherlands, Norway, the UK and Italy – this may also include lesbians or lesbian couples.

Irrespective of these legal impediments to lesbian motherhood, women's choices about reproduction and child-raising are not free from the social, religious and political influences of their communities. Currently in Europe (perhaps with the exception of Scandinavia), the freedom to live openly as a lesbian, never mind as a lesbian mother, is seen more as a privilege than a right in the eyes of the law. Looking at a few key indicators helps to put the European picture in perspective.

In all countries for which I was able to obtain definitive information, except Romania, homosexuality itself is not illegal. In many countries this change came about as a result of the need to comply with Council of Europe guidelines, not necessarily because citizens demand a change to national law. Some countries make it easy to persecute homosexuals, either men or women, with such legal provisions as the now infamous section 28 in England; lesser known cases such as prohibition of same-sex relationships in general; specifically as in Latvia making cohabitation of two lesbian or gay adults illegal; and the sketchy laws regulating public morals and decency in Italy which resulted in the 1981 imprisonment (for six months) of two women kissing on a public bench in Agrigento.

Religion also has its influence on public morals and the definition of 'family'. Those living in primarily Catholic countries like France, Italy, Spain, Portugal, Poland and Slovakia, or countries under Islamic influence like Albania, can face censure from their families and local communities for their sexuality. One person who has fought long and hard for the freedom to express her independence and sexuality is Bianca, a lively Italian lesbian mother in her mid-forties. A non-practising Catholic who had her one daughter twenty-four years ago while in a heterosexual marriage, she describes herself as a 'radical lesbian' and has spent her life acting against the establishment. Having chosen her own path, Bianca has found her life rewarding, but not easy:

I think, especially in Italy, you have to behave with great discretion. Because what you risk is too high a price to pay. I have always been active in political groups, with feminists and lesbians. I know the reality in other countries, because I travelled a lot and it is very hard to behave with this discretion. Sometimes I feel like a ghost, passing through people, like a ghost passes through a wall. But it's the only way if you want to survive here. Italy is not a good country for women, and for lesbians not at all. Catholicism influences the life of all Italians, and not only the private life but also the political situation of Italy. Catholicism says that it doesn't matter how poor you are now, what is important is what happens after death. You have no value as an individual and your life is not important so you don't have to fight to improve it.

Bianca has done much to fight such fatalistic Catholic dogma, by being politically active and attempting to live and raise her daughter in an alternative communal setting.

Catholicism is also a strong force in Poland, where an overridingly

conservative social atmosphere is strongly influenced by religious sentiment. AI is not fully legal, and at least one clinic has been challenged
on the grounds that it disposes of embryos, breaking the 1993 anti-
abortion law. It is reported that the courts regularly refuse adoption to
known homosexuals. Joanna, an out lesbian in her late twenties from
Warsaw, is the mother of two-year-old Justyna. While still in hospital
after the birth of her child, Joanna was offered money if she would
give up her baby for adoption. Originally Joanna planned to have a
child with a gay friend, but, she became pregnant by another man
after a one-night stand. Prompted by her mother, Joanna informed the
biological father of the existence of his daughter, but he professed no
interest and angrily refused to contribute in any way to the raising of
Justyna. Joanna accepts this. In fact, she doesn't feel she has much
choice as a court case over maintenance could easily escalate into a
public affair, which might threaten her custody of the child.

Despite religious and social pressures, tolerance and acceptance can
be built up by and within gay and lesbian communities or by lesbian
mothers themselves in their own neighbourhoods. Good public relations are helpful as is strength in numbers. A prime example is the
Chorlton neighbourhood of Manchester. Clare and Debbie live in a
quiet, leafy suburb in a house with a sprawling lilac bush by the front
gate and a neatly clipped lawn at the back where the children play.
Inside, the house is warm and welcoming in its untidiness. They fell
in love in 1983, when they were both twenty-two, and four years into
their 'marriage', as they describe it, they decided it was time to have
children. First Clare got pregnant and gave birth to John, then a few
years later Debbie had Kevin, both times by SI – using sperm from
donors who then had no further involvement. Clare and Debbie were
the first couple in their circle of lesbian friends to have children and
are still called upon to give advice to other lesbians interested in
becoming mothers.

Determined to provide their children with a safe place to grow up
in a 'non-traditional' family, they gave up a low-rent flat and moved
to their current home to be near other families like their own. Pinned
to a cork noticeboard in the kitchen is a flyer giving the dates of the
playgroup sessions for lesbians and their children. The number of lesbian families in the neighbourhood has grown and now Clare

describes how the local school is 'rapidly becoming THE school for lesbians' kids, mostly unknown to the rest of the parents, but I'm arguing that as a cultural minority we should be recognized as a community with our own issues within the school's equal opportunity policy'. With critical mass in the school, Clare can afford to joke,

> Mind you, lesbian motherhood is getting far too respectable for my liking here in Chorlton. We've just come back from parents evening where the place was buzzing with dykes. There's even a new girl in John's class with two mums. It's true, it's a conspiracy and we're taking over the schools, corrupting the youth and generally responsible for the decline in moral standards. YIPPEE!

2

Family **S**tructures

KATE GRIFFIN

John and Kevin have always had two mothers, as have many of their friends in the Manchester suburb where they live, so they see this as a normal family set-up. But the last thing their parents Clare and Debbie want is for the children to grow up in the lesbian version of the heterosexual nuclear family, thinking that this is the norm. 'I sometimes think this can happen in the lesbian world too, and that becomes the way the children see the world,' says Debbie. In fact different family structures abound, both in Manchester and across Europe. In lesbian, gay and heterosexual families, there are children with single mothers or fathers, children with several parents, children raised by grandparents, foster parents or friends.

How do lesbians set up their family structure and why? In the heterosexual world, family membership is often based on either legal or blood ties, whereas in a lesbian family these are often not the deciding factors. Instead, how we define family and determine its members are called into question. When a child has not one mother but two, three or more, does it make any difference who is the biological mother? Does it matter that the other mothers have neither legal nor blood links to the child? If the children were born during a previous heterosexual relationship, where does the biological father fit in? And if the children were conceived through insemination, is the donor merely an anonymous sperm supplier, or will he play a more prominent role in the life of the children?

Right from the start, Clare and Debbie chose to be a two-parent family, severing all contact with the donors. When their children were born, they were acutely aware of just how precious they were and so were keen to keep them to themselves rather than share them with other adults, including the donors. 'The children don't see themselves as having a father. That wasn't the relationship we entered into with the donors. To be fair to them, and more importantly to be fair to the kids, we've been quite clear about that from the start,' explained Debbie. 'The other thing to say' added Clare, 'is that we're both mothers to both of them. Although we've had biologically one child each, they relate to us and we relate to them both as equal. They call us both Mum. 'Mum!' 'Yeah, what?' 'Not you, the other one!'

Although John and Kevin do not differentiate between their mothers, other people do. In 1987, Clare and Debbie were the first couple in their circle of lesbian friends to have children. To their surprise, after John was born all the attention was focused on Clare as the biological mother. Debbie recalls, 'I remember one friend – I was sitting with her for about twenty minutes, talking about everything. Then Clare walked in, and she asked her all about John … That was a real shock.' It was the couple's straight friends with children who saw them as equal parents, and who accepted that parenthood was about the hard slog, the getting up in the night, not just about giving birth. At the same time, the couple have found that heterosexual women idealise their family situation. 'There's a sort of rose-tinted view of how things must be for us, because we have each other and we're two women, but we've always thought that what we don't have is a wife at home doing all the work,' Debbie laughed.

Clare and Debbie seem to paint an ideal picture of lesbian motherhood. With a successful relationship that is still going strong after thirteen years, two happy kids, a nice house, and four other lesbian families in the same street, they rarely come across anyone who questions their family set-up, in fact it can seem quite ordinary, especially in Chorlton. The main drawback is the lack of legal recognition of their family structure. One option, which they intend to pursue when they can afford it, is to go to court and apply for a residency order under the UK 1989 Children Act. The order ensures the much-desired legal recognition of the bond between a child and a significant adult who lives with the child.

Eight years after the birth of their first child, Clare and Debbie are quite sure that they created the right family structure for themselves and the children. But, like all families, situations can change and relationships break up. An anonymous lesbian from the UK wrote that after many fights with her ex-lover over parental rights and joint ownership issues, she is now sceptical about the benefits of entering into parenthood with a partner who wants equal rights. Her ex-lover went as far as to threaten court hearings if they couldn't informally agree about joint parental rights. She added that after the birth of their child, conceived using an anonymous donor, she and her ex-lover were initially

> very close knit, as parents. But as the biological parent I began to feel differences: because I was the main carer, my career didn't develop so rapidly. Eventually it pushed her away, because she was upset about being unable to conceive for herself.

When things go wrong, although court hearings may be threatened, in fact the law does not offer much help, as there is rarely any legal recognition of the relationship between the non-biological mother and child. The biological mother may feel that her ex-lover's demands are unfair, but on the other hand the non-biological mother can be left without any rights at all, dependent on the goodwill of her former partner for access to her child. And goodwill, never to be taken for granted, may be in particularly short supply after a relationship has broken up.

Kati, a 45-year-old sociologist from Finland, has experienced the trauma of family breakup, and is now able to describe her situation from a more detached viewpoint, often with humour. Although the relationship with her ex-lover is now on a fairly even keel, she often feels that her position as a separated lesbian co-mother, as she describes herself, is still rather precarious. Kati has a daughter of fourteen and a son of seven, both of whom visit her and her new lover regularly:

> Our kids spend most of their time at my former lover's (their bio-mum's) place, where my ex's new lover also lives with her two sons, but that is another story. My kids, especially the younger one, spend a lot of time at my place too. Our teenage daughter would at best not spend any time at any mum's place, and is happy having got rid of one of her three mums ...

Despite having been a full-time parent for six years before she and her lover separated, as a non-biological mother, Kati has no legal rights to her children:

> If I could do what I wanted, I would have the kids, at least the younger one, live at my place. But since there is nobody on my side, I must agree with whatever my former lover wants. Until now everything has gone well (we have been separated for

four years), but every time there is a disagreement between us, she threatens me with the possibility of not seeing my kids any more.

The relationship between Kati, her former lover and the children was never particularly straightforward. When they first met, her former lover already had a four-year-old daughter, and then they had a son together three years later:

> My daughter was 'born' to me when she was four years old. It would have been easier to become a mother with a newborn, as happened the second time, three years later. My becoming a mother with a mother with a child was a continuous triangle drama between two grown-ups and a child – jealousy in all directions. Fortunately there was a fourth woman involved, grandma, at whose place our daughter spent much time, so my ex and I could have time on our own …
>
> Becoming a mother the second time, with a newborn, was easier for me, but involved other problems. My ex stopped having sex with me after she gave birth to our son. I don't know what were her reasons, probably she could not cope with mothering an infant and an intimate relationship. But there are remaining questions: how could she cope with it before – we already had our daughter – and how can she cope with it now, with her new lover …?
>
> The story of my present lover and my son is once again the drama triangle of two grown-ups and one child, only my place in this triangle is different. If my son would live all the time at our place it would be disastrous, but fortunately he spends most of his time at my ex's place. Only I am unhappy about it. I miss him so much all the time he isn't with me.

Kati has developed very strong feelings about the rights of non-biological mothers and questions the 'myth' of blood ties or as she sees it, of the importance of genes in any discussion of kinship:

> Many lesbian bio-mothers also believe in this myth, and don't let their partners co-mother. Motherhood or parenthood is not in the blood or in the genes. Parenthood is social, not biological. Most parents just happen to be blood relatives to their children, but that doesn't say anything about their ability to parent. All adoptive and other non-biological parents can testify with me: when you learn to love a child, you can parent her or him just as the child's biological parent – or even better, because social parenthood is mostly chosen and voluntary. The secret of motherhood is in love, not in biology.

When all goes well, biological mothers who choose to involve their lover in the parenting of their children are often the first to acknowledge the importance of the role played by non-biological mothers. After all, they see the strength of that bond at first hand, and, hopefully, they benefit from the arrangement. After hearing lesbian mothers tell their stories of breakups and custody fights, it seems sensible to draw up an agreement in writing while the couple is still on good terms. Unfortunately there are no statistics to show how many lesbian mothers in Europe actually are this sensible. When love still reigns supreme, a feeling of boundless optimism can prevail over caution.

If this optimism proves unfounded, however, and the couple does break up, there are few places to turn to for advice. Often the only source of help may be friends and family, and perhaps other lesbian mothers who have already been through a similar experience. In Denmark, the social welfare authorities occasionally provide unofficial counselling to lesbian couples who are separating and help them work out their custody agreements, but there is little information about how the law has helped, if at all.

The law in the Netherlands was put to the test by Monyek and her ex-partner, who after a fairly amicable separation went to court to fight for the rights of the non-biological mother.

When they separated in 1993, after raising their son Koen together for eleven years, Monyek explains how they applied to an Amsterdam court to grant equal custody and visitation rights to the non-biological mother:

> We did this mostly because she was feeling insecure. She had helped raise him from the beginning. Since the separation, he spends half his time at her place down the block, the rest of the time with me. We feel she is still a parent.

Monyek felt they had a good chance of winning the case, as the custody law had been revised in 1985, making it possible for each partner in unmarried heterosexual couples to have legal custody of their children.

However, the Amsterdam court ruled that, because the ex-partner had no legal parental relationship to the boy, she was not eligible for custody. Monyek explains: 'The law said that the other parent did not have to be the real parent, but that it had to be possible for that person to be the real parent.' In this case, real means biological, so the person had to be a man. 'I said to the judge, you know, I can point out any man in the street and say OK, he can be the social parent [the term used for a non-biological parent]. She's the social parent, she's taken care of him from before he was born until now, and it's weird to say that anyone else can be the parent but she cannot.' According to

Monyek, the judge showed some sympathy for her argument, but still ruled against them. Monyek and her ex-partner then appealed against the verdict, arguing that the law regarding child custody would probably be revised further, and that they should both be allowed custody in anticipation of the change. They lost the appeal in June 1994.

Monyek and her ex-partner now have a good relationship, so access rights are not such an urgent issue. Despite their lack of success so far, they are determined to continue to fight the case in the future as a matter of honour, and to lead the way for other lesbian couples wanting equal custody rights.

Since the separation, both Monyek and her ex-partner have met new lovers, but Koen was not initially very welcoming, Monyek recalls:

> In the beginning, when I had a new partner, I said to him, 'Do you like her?' and he said, 'I don't know, in films and in books stepmothers are terrible.' So I said, 'Listen, you have two mothers, you have also somehow a father, that's more than enough. You can see that I would like you to like her, and if you do that's extra, but she's not an extra mother who is bringing you up.'

This gave Koen space to relate to both of his mothers' new lovers as friends, rather than feeling overburdened with parental figures.

Finding names for all the parents is an issue that frequently arises in families with more than one mother. When they were younger, Clare and Debbie's sons saw them as 'a kind of blob called Mum.' Nowadays they also call them by their first names when they want to indicate which mum they mean. In the Czech Republic, Petra's partner's daughter also calls her by her first name, but for a different reason. Petra does not consider herself a second mother nor a father to the child, even though she has cared for her since birth: 'A person only has one mother. I am not an aunty (the common title in the Czech Republic for a friend of the mother, or a childcare provider). Aunties are everywhere, women in skirts or wearing house dresses. I am like her best friend.'

A couple from Denmark who have been together for ten years and who have a twelve-year-old daughter found naming a problem at first:

> When our daughter was about two years old, started to get friends and started to talk, she had a little trouble to find out about the word 'father'. She needed a word, a name, to put on me. We tried to solve the problem by letting her call us by our first names instead of 'mama'.

When their daughter was four, the couple started a group for lesbian mothers. It was shortlived, but one major benefit was that their daughter found a name for her non-biological mother:

> The direct translation from Danish is 'with-mother' or co-mother, a woman who takes part in mothering. Suddenly she could say: this is my mother, this is my co-mother, and I am their daughter. She used it frequently, also when she started at school or other new places where she had to introduce us.

Often the problem is deeper than just finding a name. As Kati mentioned, when a mother meets a new lover and tries to introduce her into the family, jealousy can rear its head. Young children's anger at an intruder in the family who dares to take away some of their mother's precious attention can be quite visible and vocal. It takes love, time and plenty of patience to persuade a child that the perceived foe may in fact turn out to be a friend, and that an extra mother is not always such a bad thing. Other family members and friends can also be a great help, assuming of course that they themselves accept the new relationship, offering a listening ear for the child to pour out her/his often confused emotions. Spending time away from the mothers, having fun with grandmother, can also provide much-needed space for both adults and children alike.

Older children may have an equally strong, if not stronger, reaction, to the new adult in their life, but their way of showing it is often different. Rather than shouts and screams, a sulky silence is more likely from a child in her or his early teens. Italian lesbian mother Bianca's daughter Barbara, was twelve when lover Lorella appeared on the scene:

> Barbara was afraid of losing me, of course, and Lorella could not stand that I had to spend my time with my daughter. She did not say anything. Neither of the two ever said a word about this. But it was very clear. And sometimes they quarrelled about really stupid things, which were not really the problem, of course.

Bianca knew her daughter and her lover well enough to see the real reason, jealousy, lurking beneath the superficial quarrels, and decided to pacify them in her own way:

> And so – I have to admit that I behaved maybe not in a very correct way, but a practical and effective one – I told my daughter that I could not and would never leave her, that if I had to choose I would leave Lorella. Then I told my lover the same thing, that I could not and would never leave her, that if I had to choose I would leave Barbara.

Bianca herself admits that this may not have been the most honest way to treat her daughter and her lover, but she stands by her actions, as she feels that in this case the end justified the means:

> It worked. And after some years, when they brought it up, I told them, the two of them, and they really got angry with me. But I had solved the problem. I had succeeded. I was in the middle. I could not split myself in two; I was just one, so I had to do something. And it worked. But it worked because Barbara is Barbara and Lorella is Lorella and they are very nice persons, both of them. Once they were sure that I would be there for the two of them, they were no longer jealous. And then they spoke about this jealousy together, they clarified it themselves. So now, there is no problem at all. Barbara says that Lorella is her second mother, so it's no problem.

Moving on from initial problems of jealousy, another more long-term issue that arises is just how the two mothers should raise the children as a couple. The questions are endless. Who does what with the children? Who has the authority in the family? Who decides how the children are to be brought up, educated, disciplined, taught about life and how to deal with the outside world? What if there is a conflict? Does the biological mother have the final say in everything? As the following stories show, each lesbian family has to find their own answer to these questions that suits their particular situation.

Deciding how to raise the kids together can be especially tricky when both women already have children, and when they both women come from very different backgrounds, as was the case with Lena and her lover in Russia. Lena is a university teacher in her early forties, soft- spoken and eloquent. She has three children, two boys and a girl, and her lover has one son.

When they met, it was love at first sight, Lena recalled:

> This was a unique and fantastic way to get acquainted. All of my previous girlfriends I had to court for several years, as they had all been straight. Here I met my lover three years ago at virtually the first lesbian get-together I attended. Quite literally I touched her once and I realised that this was the woman for me. Then I just had to tell her. Judging from the fact that she's still with me, she believed me.

Four children between them may sound a bit of a handful, but Lena has always found it easier to have intimate relationships with women who have children.

> I don't have to explain why one time or another I don't have time. It is an objective fact that the birth of a child changes a woman's perception of time. A lesbian with children is never offended by the fact that at a particular moment my attention is

directed at a child and not at her. Childless women do get insulted.

Lena admits that she finds it a struggle to organize her hectic life, balancing her three children, her lover, her lover's child, and her work. Her monthly salary at the university is so low that she has to take on additional jobs. Bemused by a question about how she manages her childcare, she answered:

> I don't manage it. It is organized by my work, in that when I'm at work, I'm not at home. If their grandmother is not around, the children are alone. When I'm not at work I naturally spend all of my time with them, and I always spend vacations with them.

As a teacher, Lena has long holidays, the equivalent of three months.

With a child and work of her own, Lena's lover is not in a position to offer Lena much help:

> My lover and I live separately – that is, during the day we live separately; at night we live together. After work my lover spends time with her child; then she comes to my house, leaving the child with his grandmother.

Her mother disapproves of her daughter's relationship with Lena:

> She is, as is customary to say, a simple, uneducated woman, with grammar school education. She is outraged by what she knows, but can't do anything about it. Her daughter is independent, and she can't refuse to babysit as she really loves the child.
>
> It is difficult for my lover, not because of her mother's attitude, but for a bigger reason. She grew up in an environment where relationships are inhumane and cruel. She has always looked for a different kind of relating, and she found it with me. Sometimes she still shows and acts the stereotypes she grew up with – for her, inhumanity is so familiar that she doesn't notice it in certain ways. During the last three years she has changed a lot..

As well as introducing her to different ways of relating to lovers, Lena is also trying to show her a different way of relating to her son – breaking the pattern of her own childhood she is learning how to be more affectionate. Because of this, Lena is careful not to encroach on her lover's territory with her son, and avoids any kind of cross-mothering:

> I don't find it difficult to show tenderness to her son, and when we are together with all the children, say giving out treats, we don't differentiate. But I want her to be more like a mother to her son, so I leave that area open for her. I also fear that she will be jealous of me as a mother if I become a bigger authority than she, so I've never disputed any decisions regarding her son. I may say that I disapprove, but only after, never during.

Parenting two sets of children is a complex task, even if the children all like each other. When the children don't get on, it can be impossible, as was the case with one lesbian mother from the Czech Republic. 'I only have time to meet with my partner, and even that is difficult,' she explains. 'It is very complicated, the fact that our children don't like each other, and they also don't like it if we want to be together, as it means they have to be together too.' She has also found it difficult to persuade her children that two women instead of a woman and a man can constitute a family, which leads to problems with exercising authority:

> If you have a classic model of family, you deal with the conflict directly with authority. The children have to listen, whether they want to or not. But if you have two women and their children, there aren't any rules like a family.

In many eastern European countries, when the political framework collapsed the social system became much more rigid. People were clinging to rules salvaged from the wreckage of their old lives, and to structures that could protect from the new uncertainties. Not surprising, then, that rather than feel challenged to create her own rules, this tired and dejected lesbian mother does not have the strength to swim against the tide. Instead, the failed attempt to bring together two families has left her feeling utterly negative about lesbian families: 'I don't want to start another family with two women and their children. Spiritually I can't stand it'.

On the other hand, introducing a lover who does not have children into the family also involves its fair share of problems and difficulties. Christina, a film scholar in her early thirties from eastern Germany, recently moved to Bologna to live with her Italian lover, bringing her ten-year-old son Philipp with her. Her partner, Patrizia, a university teacher in her late thirties, finds that this move to family life has affected her own way of life at many levels. The first, most visible impact is on her space, as in her book-lined, carefully furnished living room children's toys are now scattered over the sofa, and the television has moved to the centre of the room:

> I have to defend my time, my space ... physical space in the house, because I was used to having more space, more time for myself. And it's more connected with a family, not with the life of a couple. So the schedule of days is different, and sometimes I have a very strong reaction against it. I'm an only child. Sometimes I give all of myself, and I feel like I give too much. In some moments I try to defend myself.

I don't think this would happen just in a relationship with a woman. I think it's part of the difficulties of being in a relationship with a child, with a woman who has a child.

Philipp has also staked out his own space, not only physically in Patrizia's apartment but also in their mental space. At a certain point in their relationship, Christina and Patrizia realized that they spent most of the time talking about Philipp rather than themselves. 'Philipp does his best to be at the centre of our conversation, when he's present or when he's absent,' Patrizia commented wryly. He also has a habit of turning up just when the couple are spending time on their own, demanding affection when he feels that his mother's love is going in another direction. 'When we are together, he often arrives at a certain moment – he has a feeling for it!'

Christina fears that so much attention from two women is not good for Philipp, as he may become very spoiled and selfish: 'What can we do to be ourselves, to protect our needs, our autonomy, against this child who asks for so much attention, and love, and money, and everything else?' The couple would like to have a larger family, to create a different dynamic. Getting pregnant again seems to be the best option, although they would rather adopt a child, but the laws in Italy and Germany do not allow this. They are also exploring other options, such as the possibility of sending Philipp to live in some sort of commune, to break the uncomfortably close bond between mother and son, that developed during the eight years Christina spent as a single mother.

Although Christina now finds it rather restricting, not all single mothers see this closeness in a negative light. Some choose to put most of their emotional energy into their child, whom they see as their full-time life partner, keeping lovers strictly part time. Having children made one lesbian mother from Denmark quite cynical about her relationships:

I see more clearly what a lesbian relationship means to me, and I don't commit myself as easily as before, because I don't want to take chances on behalf of my child. My lover has to accept the children and that I sometimes have to put them before her. So as opposite to women without children, I have other considerations of the sort of relationship I want to have with another woman. But single heterosexual women with children also have these considerations. And I don't think there are so many differences.

After having a child with a gay father, another lesbian mother from Denmark found that she was far more interested in women who also have children than in relationships, love and sex. Overwhelmed by love and affection for her baby daughter, she has experienced emotions she says she did not know were possible: 'I'm not ready yet, I just feel like a mother, not a lover.' She sometimes wonders whether she will be able to find a partner who wants to share her life the way it is now. Although she and the father decided to buy a house together that was big enough for them to share the parenting of their child and at the same time lead separate lives, much of their energy has gone into getting to know each other well enough to live together.

One lesbian mother from the UK finds that her life has been much simpler without lovers, and has chosen to concentrate on bringing up her child alone after a year of trying to co-parent within complicated relationships:

> I was involved with two women at the time I wanted to get pregnant. One didn't want me to get pregnant, the other was very excited (and over-involved) in the whole idea. The relationships followed these lines – one partner was less involved and our lives diverged quite a lot, although we are still friends and she's an important person to my child. The other relationship focused almost exclusively on my child and I had to draw boundaries about whose child she actually is – difficult struggles. My child being born tied all three of us longer into a difficult triangular situation none of us enjoyed.

After all that, being on her own came as quite a relief.

The decision to have a child, or to stay on your own and concentrate on the child rather than search for the perfect co-mother, involves various important considerations. One major factor is, of course, money. Lena felt able to have three children on her own partly because she knew she would receive additional state benefits: in Russia there is little stigma attached to being a single mother, because the state is keen to persuade women to reproduce regardless of marital status. Joanna from Poland said that she was better off on maternity leave, despite the fact that the maternity allowance is equivalent to only a quarter of the monthly salary. She normally works as a librarian, which she says is the lowest-paid profession, but while on leave she can use the time to supplement her income by teaching classes and searching for a better-paid job.

Thirty years ago in Paris, finances were not at the forefront of

Geneviève's mind when she conceived her daughter after a carefully timed one-night stand: 'I never think before I act. I was in deep shit when I had my daughter. And I often worked in two daytime jobs to give her more than the bare minimum.' Fortunately, her mother and brother rallied round and gave her support, although this also had its disadvantages. Her mother was so enthusiastic about the new addition to the family that she looked on her granddaughter as a second daughter, effectively relegating Geneviève to the role of big sister – Geneviève rebelled. Her gay twin brother's contribution, acting as a father figure, was more welcome.

Many single mums make a clear division between their love life and raising children, seeing them as two quite distinct aspects of their lives. Uli has shared apartments and the parenting of daughter Hanna, now fourteen, with other women friends ever since she left Hanna's father when Hanna was two. In Berlin, where they live, there is a visible alternative culture that encompasses a variety of family forms including communal living, so such arrangements are not regarded as particularly unusual. Uli herself, a lively redhead in her mid-thirties, is an out lesbian mother, and has given interviews on television and radio, as well as writing a book on the subject. Uli and Hanna have been living with another woman, Christiana, for the last seven years, but this story has an unusual twist to it, as Christiana moved in and became part of the family structure after her love affair with Uli had ended. Christiana helps raise Hanna, but how Hanna sees Christiana is difficult to describe: 'Mostly she is Christiana, because there is no title in this society. It depends who Hanna is telling; sometimes she says that Christiana is a friend of her mother and sometimes she says she lives with us.'

How lesbian mothers structure their family with other women and allocate roles within the family is mostly a matter of choice, and the factors influencing this choice come mainly from within their family structure – in other words, the relationship between the two or more mothers, and their relationship with the child or children. The outside world, on the whole, simply does not recognize their family structure, at least in the eyes of the law, and so does not impose on it.

Father figures are a different matter, be they ex-husbands or donors. In this respect, the outside world has more impact on the family structure, often demanding the presence of a father figure somewhere in the family, either through custody cases or as a result of general social pressures. In some countries these social pressures are so strong that women feel obliged to live with their husbands, even when they consider themselves lesbians. A Bulgarian lesbian mother in her forties, who spent ten years in a heterosexual marriage at the same time as having female partners, explained that 'women like me are forced to live in heterosexual relationships not because of financial considerations but for moral preconvictions and prejudice. They are often oppressed by parents and relatives, or they themselves are ashamed of their sexuality.' Other lesbians choose to remain with their husbands and come to a private arrangement within the existing family structure rather than break up, which may entail going public and becoming vulnerable to the criticisms of others outside the family. For these couples too, parenting and sex become disentangled over the years until they are two completely separate facets of life.

Michèle is in her early forties, and lives very amicably with her husband and two teenage daughters in a small village deep in the Belgian countryside. Although she started having lesbian relationships over ten years ago, Michèle and her husband decided not to divorce, but to live separately under the same roof. Michèle's decision was influenced initially by many different factors, and she stayed mainly for the sake of her husband and children. Financial considerations also played a role to a certain extent. 'My life and that of my children would certainly have been a lot more difficult,' she explained. 'But they aren't the only considerations. The possibility of continuing to live with their father like a "normal" family also seemed important to me.' Her environment was another factor: in a tiny village, gossip spreads quickly. Although the thought of the neighbours knowing about her private life was not a major concern for her personally, Michèle was afraid that if her lesbianism became known, this would affect the way people in the village and at the local school treated her daughters. Also, the prospect of becoming a single mother with two small children simply did not appeal to Michèle, and she did not want to move in with her woman lover. Michèle recalled that her lover had difficulty accepting this, but 'as she didn't want my children and I wouldn't have tolerated her intervention in their upbringing (which would have been inevitable, given her character), my decision was not to live with her.'

Although at the time she felt she had little choice, Michèle is now quite happy with her family arrangement. She has an excellent relationship with her husband, and she enjoys living with him as a friend, so she sees no need to change her set-up in the near future.

Such friendly arrangements that aim to meet the needs of all concerned are not so unusual, according to Romana from the Czech Republic, a teacher in her early forties with two teenage daughters. She lives in a shared household with her husband, although they separated five years ago after a fourteen-year marriage. Her attitude towards her life and choices is very matter of fact:

> We made an agreement that we wouldn't destroy anything and each of us would have their own life, so that we wouldn't harm the children. But compromise is necessary, and you never know what is hidden under the terms married, single or divorced.
>
> We decided to have a shared household as far as finances and education are concerned. It took me a long time. I had to let him know very slowly, because he thought that it would be half and half as it was in the past – bisexual. I offered him divorce and he said no, he didn't agree, because of my other qualities he thinks it isn't necessary. Now we live in a shared household, together with our partners. We don't speak about what we had, and nobody shoves it under the other's nose. There are many such marriages. After fifteen years the attraction stops. Yet people only make a big deal about the lesbian situations.

Another lesbian mother from the Czech Republic finds that it is much harder to cope with her ex-husband, however. She still lives with him, but according to her, this is not through choice. He refuses to move out, even though he has been ordered to do so by the courts. She described how their 17-year marriage has been one long history of power struggles and abuse as her husband knew about her lesbianism from the start and used it against her. She feels that he manipulated her into marriage, and then into staying with him, first by getting her pregnant against her will and then threatening to take their two children, now in their teens, if she divorced him. With support and encouragement from her girlfriend, she finally succeeded in divorcing him six years ago, citing his behaviour as a reason, not her sexuality:

> After many years of fights and disagreements, the court still has not made a decision on how many times the father would meet the children. It still isn't clear. The

decision will be made after the division of the household. During the past two years he has only taken care of the children for one weekend. He is abusing this situation to the maximum.

In the Czech Republic there is one known case of a lesbian mother going to court to fight for custody, having cited her lesbianism as grounds for the divorce. She had to undergo a battery of psychological and other tests, but in the end she was awarded custody on the grounds that she and her new female partner were likely to be better parents for the ten-year-old boy than the recently remarried father and his new wife.

Custody cases can make family life impossible. One lesbian mother from Italy told of a long and arduous two-year battle for the custody of her son, now ten, against a father who seemed to have everything on his side. Although willing to be interviewed, even four years later she is still very careful to conceal her identity for fear of possible repercussions. While the custody case was under way, the shadow of the father loomed large over the family. During that period, she hardly ever saw her son, as he spent most of his time with his father. She is convinced her ex-husband's hostility towards her affected the child, so that her son was uneasy about coming to stay with her and her new lover. In the beginning, the father was a dominant figure in the child's eyes who did everything right, she explained, while she was portrayed the 'crazy person', and it took a long time for her to have any influence over her son.

Her lover also found it hard to establish a relationship with the child. Faced with this commanding male figure who wielded all the power, she felt that she lacked parental authority, being young (in her early twenties), female, a student and a lesbian. Despite these difficulties, the tale ended on a happier note. Having finally agreed virtual joint custody with the father, they were able to start building a life together, mother, lover and son: 'We moved house, we came to live here and he got his own room; so that's when family life started, nearly four years ago. He's got his space, his life, and his cat, a magical cat.'

Sometimes lesbian mothers feel that the odds are so stacked against them that it is not worth going to court. One UK lesbian mother recalled how she was 'browbeaten and blackmailed into giving up custody' before the case came to court, when she and her husband divorced nine years ago. Her social situation compared very unfavourably with her ex-husband – he was a partner in an insurance booking company with a three-bedroomed house; she was unemployed and living in a bedsit. She describes how he also used her lesbianism as an argument, threatening to turn the children against her. She felt it was hopeless to fight, and so agreed to let the boys live with their father for most of the year.

Even when custody is not an issue and the father has long since left the scene, he can return to haunt a lesbian mother wishing to take advantage of her freedom, as Christina from eastern Germany found out when she wanted to start family life with her lover in Italy. Although the father's contribution to the family may not have extended much further than sowing the seed, fathers' rights are firmly embedded in the legal structure. Christina has full custody of her ten-year-old son, Philipp. Her ex-husband pays living costs and has the right – which she says he has never exercised – to visit the child. Christina's only contact with him has been through a children's rights agency, which ensures the continuation of the maintenance agreement. But when Christina and Philipp decided to change back to her maiden name, her ex-husband took offence and threatened to stop payments:

> At that moment, my biggest fear was of losing my child. I never told my ex-husband how I live – why should I? I saw him twice in the last five years. But now, dealing with the administration and writing official papers, I tried to hide what I am – a lesbian.

Christina had every reason to be cautious. In Germany there is currently a campaign to change the law regarding parental rights. Fathers want more rights over their children, and thus more control over the mothers, even when they live apart: 'So in this case I wouldn't be able to move to Italy with my child, to live with my lover – lesbian lover! – because the biological father would say no.' In divorce and custody proceedings, an increasing number of judges do not take into account a mother's lesbianism. But the idea of shared custody has become popular with the youth welfare department and with judges. Shared custody does not concern the actual childcare, but the authority to make decisions such as which school a child is going to attend. If a lesbian mother is doomed to this variant and the child stays with her, her former husband will have numerous ways to intervene legally in her future life. With the forthcoming reform of family law, shared custody will probably be the rule. Christina is angry and frustrated by the unfairness of her situation:

> Is this the way? That a man – who never lived with the child, never really took care of him – can control my life for twenty or more years, although I divorced him ten years ago and never met him again? It's such a serious danger for our lives, for our children, for ourselves.

For lesbian mothers, custody cases usually involve submitting themselves to the judgement of the outside world in the form of a judge. The question of choice is removed. Occasionally, however, lesbian mothers have agreed to grant the father custody after the separation or divorce in the belief that the children would prefer this arrangement. One lesbian mother from Norway explained: 'I didn't want to break them up from both his and my family. Also they live in the same house as they always have, and play with their old friends, and go to the same school.' The main problem with this arrangement is that she lives a seven-hour drive away from her children, and so cannot see them as often as she would like.

Breaking with the conventional view of the mother taking primary responsibility for the day-to-day care of a child, some lesbian mothers may risk disapproval from the society around them and choose to let their child live with the father most of the time, coming to visit during the holidays instead, when they can enjoy each other's company to the full. Her reasons may include having a stressful job which involves long hours or a lot of travelling, or moving to another country where the child would have to learn a new language and adapt to a completely different way of life. Furthermore, if the father has a second family with other children, the child may prefer to be with her or his siblings for most of the time. Extended families, in which various parents are involved in raising the children, can find co-ordinating all the different access visits extremely complicated!

In contrast to lesbian mothers who have to negotiate custody agreements with sometimes co-operative, sometimes not so co-operative, ex-husbands or male lovers, lesbians who decide to have children by SI tend to have much more control over the agreement with the father or the donor. Often the amount of time the donor is to spend with the child, if at all, is decided before the child is born, leading to fewer arguments later. A lesbian mother from Denmark who has arranged for the donor, a gay male friend, to have an equal share in the custody of her son sees a great advantage in such an arrangement: 'Being a lesbian mother the way I have chosen leaves a great part of the responsibility for the childcare with the father, and I think that it is easier for him to take this responsibity because we don't live together.'

Despite prevailing social attitudes that a child needs a mother and a father, many lesbian mothers would question this belief. Some, like Clare and Debbie, feel that their children can manage perfectly well without a father. Others, while unconcerned by the lack of a father figure, still ponder on whether male role models would be helpful to their children, especially sons. Patrizia thinks that Philipp 'has a lack of male role models at home or around. A large part of Christina's community is a female community of friends.' Christina agrees: 'Yes, there is a strong longing for a male part in his world, because he has enough female parts. But I don't feel it as a lack. More an attraction, I would say.' When given the chance, Philipp enjoys playing and talking with young men, usually the couple's male friends or acquaintances.

Philipp's ideas about his father are linked to his views on male culture in general. Patrizia recounted one episode:

> We were on vacation, driving in the car, and suddenly he said, 'oh mama, I love you very much', and 'Patrizia, I love you too'. Then he said, 'I don't love my father very much, but one day he will come back with a big red car'.

She commented that this picture of the absence of a father is perhaps more connected with what he feels he cannot get from them, as two women. He sees big red sports cars as part of the male culture, so he connects this male fantasy figure with consumption, 'probably because he sees a lot of his friends' fathers buying new cars' she added. Their main concern is that the absence of his father may lead Philipp to idealize father figures, equating the lack of a father with other gaps he perceives in his life. More contact with men might help dispel the belief that a father would be the answer to all his problems.

Philipp's interest in young men has been a problem for Patrizia in her search for a recognized role in their family structure. 'Who is the other woman?' she asked. 'She's not a mother, she's not a father, she's a friend of the mother, but she also has responsibilities in terms of education, connections, life,' yet socially she is nothing. Patrizia admits, 'in the meantime I have been a little jealous when Philipp was very attracted by young men, because I couldn't, well ... I can rationalize everything, but my reaction was a very unconscious reaction: "What do I have less than young men?" '

Kati from Finland, the non-biological mother of two children born by SI, does not have problems with feeling inadequate where men are concerned, mostly because she has had great difficulty in introducing male figures into her children's lives. She tells the story of her failure with evident amusement:

> I have desperately tried to organise contacts for both of my kids with male persons, since they have both spent their lives in entirely female surroundings (grandma, first two and now three or four moms, female teachers, female daycare personnel) but all my attempts during the last ten years have failed.
>
> My gay male friends, whom we chose to become godfathers to our son, have shown no interest in him. All my attempts with other gay males have also failed – kids simply do not belong to the gay male world. I don't know any straight men in person, except relatives. Six months ago I brought my son to the Boy Scouts, one of the reasons being to allow him to be in an all-male surrounding. Last week there was disappointing news: they had reorganized the boy scouts, and the two nice young men who were guiding them had taken on another group of older boys, and my son's group is taken care of by two nice young women. I don't know who was more disappointed, my son or me. Now I'm only waiting for news from the sports club that they will also change to a female coach ...

Kati is very clear why she wants male figures in her children's lives:

> I do not believe in the bullshit of the importance of a father figure for bringing up the children. I simply think it is good for children to know there are usually two genders in our western culture, even if lesbian families are mostly one-gendered. When my son learnt to speak, the words 'woman' and 'adult' were synonymous for him. I think it is no bad idea, but I think it is no bad idea either to tell him the rest of the world doesn't think so.

3

The World Outside

LISA A. MULHOLLAND

Having children shakes up the life of a parent. Schedules shift to fit the decrees of the newest family member, sleeping-in becomes a dream and adult conversation tends to revolve around bottles and bodily functions. Having a strong, helpful family or support group can make the transition to parenthood easier, but having children doesn't just bring lesbian mothers into contact with family and friends; the outside world comes creeping in before, during and after the birth or adoption. All of a sudden a strikingly butch lesbian can become, to the public eye, a heterosexual mum-to-be. She finds other (pregnant) women smiling at her on the bus and eyeing her body, this time without a sexual sparkle. Older women may feel free to stroke her belly while starting up a conversation, offering stories and advice from their own birth experiences and sometimes asking about the father-to-be. Families of origin may turn up, either to scold or rejoice, or perhaps a bit of both.

An expectant co-mother, however, not showing her condition in a physical form often experiences a very different reaction. Unless she claims and reclaims her parenthood, she may be left out of the process and ignored by medical staff, her partner's parents, friends and certainly older mums on the bus. Being treated as a parent by the biological mother helps at home, but others, like the co-mother's employer or even close friends may not recognize her responsibilities toward the child and be reluctant to help with time off or other assistance.

Lesbians have the power to knock down stereotypes right and left as they approach and enter parenthood. Yet, aware that their sexuality might be putting an added pressure on their children, many lesbian mothers first think long and hard about having children, and second, carefully consider not so much how to *change* society but how to *protect* their offspring. Encouraging trends were evident in the stories collected for this book and in other, more scientific studies, proving what we already knew – that lesbian parents are just as likely to have happy, healthy children as anyone else (if not more so!). When parents feel comfortable about their own sexuality and are able to live with at least a modicum of freedom and pride, children seem able to take that strength out into the world they face each day.

Lesbian mothers, like other responsible parents want what is best for their children. Deciding just what constitutes 'best' is one of the tasks of parenting. Reacting to individual situations and pressures, the ways in which European lesbian parents present themselves both to their own children and to the outside world is neither rigid nor fixed and there is no winning formula. Women chose strategies that they felt were appropiate to the moment at hand or that develop into long-term goals. Many initially have the comfort of the children in mind, yet realize that momentary comfort doesn't always lead to strength. Mothers, co-mothers and children can all face the continual process of coming out in schools, playgrounds, after-school care, parent association meetings and hospitals, etc. Each family must decide the limits, if any, to their coming out and determine the best way to present themselves to their particular world.

Sometimes it is difficult for lesbian mothers to be open with their young children who might say the wrong thing at the wrong time and so 'out' the parents in a difficult or dangerous situation. Russia, for example, is not currently the safest place in Europe for lesbian mothers or their children. Lena's two older children (a boy of thirteen and a girl of nine) know about her sexuality. The son surprised her in an embrace with another woman and the daughter realized it by herself. Luckily the children are shrewd enough to know that they must be careful. 'My son realizes it is dangerous for him to say his mother is queer,' reports Lena. 'My daughter maybe whispers with her best friend, but I don't know. It is dangerous for them to discuss it with other children, because in their families they have a negative attitude to gay and lesbian relationships.' She worries about finding a balance between being honest and protecting the children from 'the aggressive heterosexual world'. The difficulty as Lena sees it is in 'conveying the complexity of life – the world inside the home with the mother is one thing, the world outside is another'. The dreams that this lesbian has are unreachable, and the possible costs too high:

> Any ideas I might have for changing my life I do not make real, because I would put my children in more danger than they already are. I cannot speak openly under my last name as a lesbian, because I am afraid that my children will be harassed. I can't open a business because I fear that in that case my children will be used to harrass me – I would be vulnerable to racketeers and put my children in danger of being kidnapped or killed. I can't leave this country to go to a safer country, because of my mother who is used to living here and wouldn't want to move. So I can only dream ...

Mothers may also fear that questions about their sexuality might arise if they have to go to court for custody battles. When her son was four, an anonymous lesbian mother from Italy decided to separate from her ex-husband and move in with her lover, but as her ex-husband was aware of her lesbian relationship, she had no negotiating power as regards custody. Her ex-husband and three-quarters of the local judges are involved in the Communione Liberazione, a Catholic integralist movement, so she knew right from the start that if her lesbianism became known in court, she ran a high risk of losing access to her son altogether. When the case first went to court, and without the services of a lawyer, she describes how she was tricked by her ex-husband's lawyers into signing an agreement that awarded full custody to the father, and allowed her to see her son for only a few hours every week.

After a long search, she found a lawyer (through the Italian lesbian and gay association Arci Gay Arci Lesbica) who was willing to take on her case and appeal against the agreement. Her lawyer advised her against fighting for equal custody rights with the father, as she did not want to risk aggravating the father and losing the little she had already gained. Instead, through careful negotiations they managed to change some clauses in the act of separation, with the result that her son could come and live with her for almost half of the year.

Although not officially recognized as a reason for restricting custody in most Western countries, many women fear to have their lesbianism brought up in court. Reports from Denmark, Germany, Ireland, the Netherlands, Norway, Poland, Sweden and Switzerland, however, claim that lesbianism is not normally given much weight before the judge. In other countries such as Portugal, Serbia, Belgium and Italy, lesbians find that their sexuality is held up as evidence that they are unfit to be good parents. In Portugal, one lesbian mother said that because 'lesbian' is such a common insult hurled against women by their husbands when fighting for custody, judges take no notice of such accusations.

Although threatened neither by custody nor kidnapping, two UK mothers caution their children about being too open for fear of adverse reactions. They each have daughters about seven years old, and one also has a nine-year-old son. Both find that their support groups and friends tend to be heterosexual mothers and each has found it necessary to caution her children about being too public about their mother's sexuality:

> My daughter knows not to talk about it at school and she also knows which of her friends have mums who are the same as hers. Occasionally she gets confused. For example, she thought she couldn't say 'Ms' at school. She thought it was the same as lesbian.

The other woman also explains to her children the need for keeping quiet: 'I advise them not to talk openly outside the home, because other people wouldn't understand.'

Sometimes it isn't only outsiders who don't understand. Franta, a twelve-year-old Czech boy, is bewildered by the changes in his family structure. He lives with his divorced mother and father in the same household. Home life is not ideal as his father is abusive towards the children and his former wife and refuses to move out. Franta also has difficulty understanding his mother's relationship with another woman. At school he learns that homosexuals are 'disgusting' and cause 'problems in society'. At home he tries to reconcile his mother's sexuality with what he hears from his peers, who equate 'homo' with pervert. His mother, Alena, recounts his verbal musings as they sat together on the sofa one evening. ('Tepla' is a word which directly translates as 'warm' but also acts as an ugly slang reference to lesbian) '"Mother are you really tepla?" "Yes," he answered himself, snuggling closer, "You are really warm."' Alena says she has tried repeatedly to explain her relationship and homosexuality, but can't compete with the societal influences she is up against.

Eleven-year-old Honza, also a Czech, has no such problems discussing his new two-women household and the greater implications with both his mother Renata and her partner Vera, as his mother recounts:

I have explained to my child, in accordance with his age, what it means to be homosexual and heterosexual. I told him that being homosexual means living together with a person of the same sex – aunty with aunty, man with man – and that there are fewer of these people than the others and that this is quite normal in some states, but in our country it has only now begun to develop. Because these people are so rare, the others can be bad and cruel with them and this is unjust.

Armed with this information, Honza is able to make his own decisions about who to tell and who not. Ready to accept Vera in his private life, he has worked out his own solution for the public representation. Renata remembers one particular occasion:

He drew a Christmas card for my partner who was abroad and he mentioned 'aunt', but he never calls her aunt. I asked about it and he said, 'Not everybody has to know about it'. He is not the type of child who tells everything to anybody at first sight. He thinks about what he is going to say. He is not afraid to invite his friends home and they don't ask him about my partner, what she is doing here. They just don't get the idea, because he doesn't mention it.

Lesbian mothers like Renata and Alena find that both their children and their children's peers deal with the situation of lesbian parents differently depending on their age or stage of life. The definition of parents for very young children focuses more on 'Who takes care of me?' and 'Who takes care of you?' than any other criteria. As children grow and learn more about the biological aspects of parenting, the questions become more science-based: 'How did I come to be in this family?' and 'How are two mothers biologically possible?' Adolescents move on to the next stage: while dealing with their own changing sexuality, they question that of their parents and the other adults they know.

A number of mothers told stories of how open their eight-or nine-year-old children were or are as far as being out at school or with play-mates was concerned. One Danish lesbian mother, Monyek in the Netherlands, and Clare and Debbie in the UK all have sons who found their peers a bit 'stupid' for failing to understand how anyone could have two mothers. A single lesbian mother from the UK tells of how comfortable her daughter feels with her mother's sexuality.

She went through a phase of telling all her peers and inviting them to become dykes, too! She was very impressed by dykes and saying she was one too (at about nine years old). She has quietened down a bit and is seen as outrageous and weird at school. She talks to me admiringly of dykes, but is not particularly curious about sex except to see if she can tease me.

Depending on the policy of the family as a whole and their stage in life, children make their own decisions on how to present themselves to their peers. Many factors come into play, ranging from culture, religion and the socio-economic background of the child's neighbourhood to more personal factors such as self-esteem, a particular teacher or bout of teasing. Regardless of the specific situation, it is clear that 'coming out' is not a process restricted to gays and lesbians, but also represents an integral part of life for children of lesbian mothers. As Monyek points out, 'You don't spend the whole day making announcements like: "Hello, I'm Monyek, I'm a lesbian" and neither do children (unless they are nine!), 'I don't think they talk so much about it, ' says one Danish mother with three children under ten. 'There is no reason to explain so much, because all the children from the kindergarten and classes have visited our home at the children's birthdays and we all participate at parties at the institutions. But they don't declare "My mother is a lesbian."'

Children's criteria and methods of coming out may not be clear to their parents, but they must make their own judgements. Talking about their elder son John, Clare and Debbie had this to say:

> It is quite clear that, like us, our older son has different levels of coming out. He'll tell some people the whole thing. With others it is difficult and he tells what he thinks that they will understand. He often says 'well, I won't bother telling her 'cos she is stupid' or 'I'm not really friends with them so they don't know'. But, with others he tells, it doesn't seem to be too much of a thing. Most of his friends seem to know.'

Clare and Debbie try to help both children whenever they can. 'Our technique when they went to a new school was not to tell people right away,' explained Debbie, 'but just make no secret of it. You could see people and friends of the kids at school gradually realize, so it feels like you've got a bit of control over when they realize.' Having control over one's own coming out is a technique that Sylvie (in France) taught to her own child more than twenty-five years ago.

> I have never declared my homosexuality except to people with whom I had sufficient contact to know that they were not homophobic, so the reaction has always been positive. My daughter as always behaved in the same way. She talks about it with certain friends or colleagues, whose points of view she knows in advance.

Those mothers who are willing and able to be open with their children can offer guidance, suggestions and direct help. They frequently put a lot of thought into how to approach or come out to others, considering not only themselves but how to make the way clearer for the children. Some drop hints until people realize by themselves, others introduce themselves to teachers or childcare providers in advance, making the situation clear and emphasizing that the co-mothers are equally responsible for the child in question.

John and Kevin are also lucky enough to have parents who are willing and able to discuss the issues of a two-mother family. Both parents have been open with their children from birth. The mothers feel that their community in Chorlton is a supportive one which allows them and their boys to be as public about their lives as they could wish to be:

> Anyone who is significant or important knows. And again for the kids, I think that they know this as well. They don't have to carry any sort of secrecy about it. It makes it safer for them if there aren't things that are secret, especially while they are young.

One Danish mother and her lover co-parent two boys aged sixteen and seven, conceived by SI with unknown donors. They live in a small Danish village and are well known to their fellow villagers. Their technique for dealing with other parents is simple. 'I have been careful to invite both playmates and their parents to our home,' she explains. 'My sons have several playmates all allowed to come to our house, and to have my sons visiting them. When we and our home are well known people do not get scared and then they do not have to react negatively. ' She also chooses her phraseology with her audience in mind: 'Most people around us know. In front of old-fashioned people we do not use the words lesbian or homosexual, but they all know we are partners. It is up to them to guess if we are sexual partners, too.'

Children who enter the world in a heterosexual family which later breaks up do not necessarily see their mother's homosexuality as a normal part of their lives. Mothers may also choose not to discuss it at all. One forty-year-old Bulgarian interviewee has never discussed her sexuality with her son, who is now nineteen years old. She divorced her husband when her boy was ten years old and currently has a girlfriend with whom she hopes to live after her son begins his military service. She describes how she had female partners even during her marriage, and thinks her son is probably aware of her current relationship. However, she is pleased that he doesn't pose 'uneasy' questions. She isn't comfortable enough with her own sexuality to come out directly to her child, although she admits that all indications are that he would react positively or at least neutrally.

Taking information from the country profiles into consideration, this Bulgarian lesbian seems more likely to face more homophobia than, say, her counterpart in Denmark. At the same time, lesbian mothers all across Europe are not immune to internalizing anti-homosexual sentiment. This internalized homophobia can make women hesitant to be open, even in situations which seem relatively 'safe'. One mother from the UK says, 'I am very confident about my mothering skills and other mothers often admire my relationship with my daughter.' Yet she admits, 'I feel a bit scared about coming out in case they think my daughter might be a bad influence on their children.' Then, when other mothers do learn about a lesbian parent's sexuality there is the constant pressure to defend one's abilities or the right of lesbians in general to have children. A Danish lesbian says: 'I sometimes feel that I have to be a better mother than others', while a Norwegian lesbian expresses the same doubt: 'I feel that I have to prove that I am a decent mother.'

Sometimes having children exerts great pressure on relations that are already strained. Although limited, we collected a few stories about losing friends or relations over the issue of having children. A Danish mother reported, 'Most friends don't care. I lost one friend because she thinks homosexuals should not have children.' All in all she isn't upset, 'I have only had a few negative reactions. But of course I avoid people who mind me being a lesbian. I don't see it as a problem.' A lesbian from Norway has experienced similar reactions:

> Before having a child my sexuality was more or less OK for everybody. They didn't exactly shout it out. But today I feel more pressure from them to hide my sexuality and to be heterosexual 'because of the child'. Still, they love and respect us too much to cut the relationship, so we have a lot of support from them.

On the other side of the coin, lesbians can also find that being a mother brings them certain benefits from society, requested or not. 'Being a mother is fine, deeply good, and I think we look more like "normals" in hetero eyes', says one mother of two. She is supported by Christina, a German living in Italy, who finds that she feels 'a resonance from society' about her motherhood: 'That I am the mother of a son is more than only to be a woman.' Lesbians who have children may bask in the glow of societal approval on occasion and they may find that their primary friendships and support groups shift away from lesbian circles to include a strong base of other mothers, who are frequently heterosexual.

Sometimes those approving heterosexual mothers are their own. Having a grandchild frequently precedes a truce between warring families of origin. The parents of an adult lesbian may or may not be in favour of her lifestyle or the gender of her partner, but few are willing to miss out on the next generation. Polish Joanna has never had a direct conversation with her mother about her sexuality, but when they fight, her mother accuses her of having only 'faggots and lesbians' for friends. At the same time, Joanna's mum let her know early on that it was fine with her if Joanna ever became a 'single' mother and currently offers lots of help with childcare. Joanna happily admits, 'The child is the best present I could give my mother.' A Danish lesbian agrees, finding that although her mother isn't comfortable with her sexuality, with SI, she isn't willing to break from the new family and miss out on seeing her two-year-old granddaughter: 'My mother has to get used to it, but she loves her grandchild.'

In the UK, Debbie's parents have had a lot of trouble adjusting to the way she has chosen to live. They are worried about the neighbours' opinions, to the extent of forbidding visits, yet they aren't able to turn their backs completely on their daughter's family. She explains:

> I don't think my family would be where they're at now with me if I hadn't had the kids. It isn't a reason for having them but it's sort of given my parents a handle. This way they can ignore the sexual side. There is more communication and a better relationship than I had before. It is on their terms and I know damn well that if we didn't have kids our relationship would still be out in the wilderness.

Grandchildren may act as a bridge connecting parents and their adult lesbian children. Those same children can also bring together their mothers and other, heterosexual, women.

Sometimes lesbian mothers find more acceptance from heterosexual parents than childless lesbians. One lesbian mother from the UK finds her friendship circle has straightened out:

> I had hardly any heterosexual women friends before, and now I have lots. I'm close to my daughter's child-minder and to lots of other women who are mothers of my daughter's friends. It's been a welcome broadening experience and the mutual sup-

port has been invaluable. I have far more in common a lot of the time with heterosexual mothers than with lesbians who are not mothers. The only problem is the
men who are connected with the heterosexual women, but mostly I manage to
avoid them.

'We are not very different from other mothers,' muses an anonymous
parent from Denmark. 'Even though I am not our son's biological
mother I love to talk about him, discuss where you can buy the best
baby clothes, etc. I think it has brought us into the parent's group.'
Lesbian mothers used words like 'links', 'bonds', 'channels', 'something in common' when discussing their changing relations with heterosexual women. Renata from the Czech Republic explains:

Being a mother is an advantage. I feel it is influential in relations with heterosexual women. People take me as an equal: I have a child, the same or similar worries
and experiences, I am completely the same as they are.

'I haven't had a lot of time for contacting others except for my
mother and baby group,' explains one Danish woman with a two-
year-old daughter by SI. 'They are all heterosexual women. It's always
easier to talk with mothers when you have become a mother yourself.'
Renata and other mothers of various nationalities found that the issue
of lesbianism was accepted, tolerated or even avoided altogether
when accompanied by motherhood: 'having a child can be a social
"smoke screen" that gives you another acceptable identity, less threatening than the obvious lesbian lifestyle!'

AI and SI for single or lesbian women is seen by some in society as
part of that 'threatening' lifestyle. Popular for some time now in western Europe, insemination can pose difficulties for lesbians and their
children when it comes to explaining their family situations at school.
Youngsters who can't name their fathers (anonymous donors) may be
teased or even tormented by schoolmates who find the situation
strange if not impossible. Having peers in the same position provides
a great deal of support, and having mother(s) who are able and willing to discuss it with them or classmates is even more helpful. Koen,
Monyek's son, had the whole thing carefully thought out and, when
younger, was able to educate his friends as his mother recalls:

At primary school he was talking very openly to his friends and was explaining
things. In the beginning they accepted what he said, then they began to know the
technology and then they thought 'Jesus, how is it possible?' ... He explained 'Of

course I have a father, but my mothers love each other so they live together and my father, well he is a friend and you need that for a seed …

Monyek found it funny just how proud he was of his own beginnings.

Other AI and SI children can feel the necessity to educate classmates, or even stand up and aggressively protect their mothers' methods of getting pregnant. One respondent from the UK told the story of her eight-year-old daughter:

My child sometimes has to defend the possibility that someone cannot have a father. She finds it hard that she has to, sometimes with children she doesn't know very well, but it is more biology than sexuality that they discuss at her age. I think she discusses not having a father with other kids who don't live with their dads. I don't think that she's quite at an age where sexuality is a big issue for her or her friends yet, and other lesbian couples with children or women with SI donor babies are very normal for her.

Still other children ask for their mothers to explain the procedure to their friends. Explaining the mechanics of SI or AI to a classroom of giggling children may not be everyone's cup of tea, but giving up the responsibility of explanation must come as a relief to a child.

Most mothers who told their stories were able to report that children who had the support of their parents regarded their situations as completely normal. Those raised in openly lesbian households from birth or an early age seem to have the best time of it, going so far as to consider the children from so-called 'traditional' homes strange, particularly if they reacted with confusion to the two-mother home situation. Looking over the collected stories, non-biological co-mothers who are able to take an active role from birth are accepted by their children and their children's classmates with little or no problem. Debbie has had the fun of watching the process in action:

When I was picking them up the other week, one of the kids in his class came running along with her big brother, who was a couple of years older. She ran up to John and said, 'John, John, you've got two mums haven't you?' He said, 'Yeah' and she said, 'See!' and they both ran off. It is just a fact.

Honza doesn't feel as comfortable as John evidently does about being open with his eleven-year-old classmates. Once however, the young Czech boy did have a slip of the tongue in the presence of a schoolmate. Describing his weekend, Honza said 'I went on a trip with Vera and my mother.' When the other child asked, 'Who is Vera?', he gulped and said casually, 'Uhhmm, she is a woman'. The friend responded 'Oh, that is normal nowadays'. The reaction of Honza's young friend may happily reflect a trend that is growing in Europe. Many women who responded to the questionnaire, especially those from Denmark, found that being open was met sometimes with surprise and occasionally disapproval, but more frequently with shrugged shoulders and minimal reaction. Good experiences lead to greater confidence. A Danish lesbian parent agrees: 'Most people know about our family situation. At the boy's creche there is openness and nobody looks upon it as perverse or unnatural. I think the acceptance of others has a lot to do with the way you present yourself.' Another Danish lesbian became a co-mother to her lover's daughter when the child was one and a half years old. The girl knows about her mothers' sexuality and has two classmates with similar families. The co-mother is active in many aspects of her child's life and says, 'At the after-school childcare I, the non-biological, non-anything parent joined the parent's council and nobody thought it strange, or never showed it anyway.' One of their compatriots has a similar approach and also tries to live her life as she wants.

> Some people may think my way of living is strange or even 'perverted', but because I talk about my life openly, no one tells me they think that it is wrong or strange. I have never tried to hide. If anyone asks about my private life, I simply tell them how it is. If they don't like my answer they shouldn't have asked, but I think that is their problem.

Not every lesbian mother is lucky enough to live in the relative openness of Denmark, however, and they and their children have to assess their personal situations and safety before setting or removing limits on what they will tell others. When the socio-political situation is such that secrecy is necessary, or when custody battles hover threateningly on the horizon mothers must make choices about when and how much knowledge to entrust their children or their own friends and co-workers with. These situations can be hard and unfair on everyone involved, but let us hope that soon the majority of Europe's population will react in the same way as Honza's friend.

4

Identity and Community
KATE GRIFFIN

> I don't think motherhood can be classified as lesbian or
> non-lesbian, motherhood is a category unto itself.
> (Lena, Russia)

Questions of identity and community are circular and interconnected, leading from one into the other and back again, with similar issues resurfacing across Europe in different contexts. How a lesbian mother identifies herself – as lesbian, mother, lesbian mother or lesbian and mother – influences her position within the lesbian community, while at the same time the prevailing attitudes toward motherhood within that community influence how she defines herself.

In Russia, 'lesbian mother' is not a label that sticks easily, as sexuality and reproduction are seen as two different and often unconnected aspects of a woman's life. Many women become mothers when they are young, often in their early twenties or before. The desire to have children is not tied to expectations of marriage or of having a male partner – for Russian women, having children is what some women may choose to do at some point in their life, whereas having a husband may not be part of that choice. Many lesbians had children when they were young, either before or after they embraced their lesbianism. The lack of a partner, male or female, is not necessarily seen as a problem, as there is no social stigma attached to single parenthood. At a practical level, many women continue to live with their parents even after the children are born, and so it is not unusual for grandmothers to look after the children while mothers go out to work.

Just as motherhood is not divided into lesbian and non-lesbian, similarly many Russian lesbians do not divide themselves into mothers and non-mothers. Lesbians at the local lesbian and gay organization in Moscow started to organize a series of meetings specifically for lesbians. At the beginning, the focus was on issues related to lesbian motherhood, as most of the lesbians were also mothers, but this division seemed artificial and the meetings soon opened out to include all lesbians, with or without children. Issues such as coming out, although particularly important for mothers because of the need to take into consideration the effect on the children, are relevant and of interest to all lesbians, so the organizers saw no need to exclude non-mothers from the group.

Mothers and non-mothers mix easily in lesbian circles in Moscow. But what *is* the lesbian community? In Russia, this is hard to define. There are different groups of lesbians who meet in different places for different reasons, but there are no prevailing attitudes or ideologies that link them together or that could be used to mark the boundaries of the lesbian community.

Germany provides a striking contrast. In West Berlin in the 1970s and early 1980s the lesbian community had very clear beliefs, adherence to which defined who was a member of the community and who was not. One of the popular ideas of the time was that women should rebel against the patriarchy by refusing to do reproductive work for men. As it was the same women who propounded these ideas and who organized most of the lesbian events in Berlin, it was difficult for lesbians to escape this predominant ideology. Lesbian mothers felt estranged from most of the lesbians they met, as they had broken these rules. It was difficult to find a partner, the lesbian meeting points offered no childcare, male children often had no access to social events and pregnant lesbians were despised by the majority for having slept with a man. Above all, there was no forum for discussion of the differences between the situation of lesbian mothers and straight mothers. Years later such feminist and lesbian theory was attacked for having ignored anyone who was not young, white, independent, middle class, academic and career-oriented; thus groups for lesbian mothers and older lesbians began to appear.

When the rules about who belongs to the community are so strict and identities are rigidly defined, it is difficult for lesbian mothers to embrace both aspects of their identity. Although lesbian mothers are now more integrated into the lesbian scene in Germany, Uli Streib (an out lesbian mother and author from Berlin) says she still encounters 'discussions or opinions in the lesbian community that you are a wrong lesbian if you had a heterosexual life and a child'. Uli had her daughter in a heterosexual relationship before she came out as a lesbian and is now very wary of being labelled simply as a mother: 'The problem I had with groups of lesbian mothers was that I refused to say I'm a mother, and that was the definition – lesbian mothers. I said I am a lesbian, but with a child.' Uli believes that identifying as a 'mother' would suppress all the other facets of her identity, that 'as a mother you can leave the lesbian off, mother is in the centre of the definition, and all the other things I am – a woman, a lesbian, a lover – disappear; I have to be a mother … nothing else.' Uli has written two books on lesbian motherhood (see Bibliography). She also leads workshops for lesbian mothers, both actual and potential.

Christina from eastern Germany, a film scholar in her early thirties, also made the transition from heterosexual mother to lesbian in the Berlin scene. Although she does not reject her identity as mother like Uli, Christina feels that her two identities are in conflict: 'I would describe my situation as a lesbian mother as "sitting between all chairs". I am like Mary, a single mother with a son, but I am also a young autonomous lesbian.' She feels that her motherhood has inhibited the development of other aspects of her identity and has been a restricting factor in the way she has led her life, especially during the years she spent as a single mother without a partner. Having felt frustrated by her isolation from the lesbian community in Berlin, she is sharply aware of the different lifestyles of lesbians with children and those without:

> I would like to be a childless lesbian too. 'To be free, autonomous, work, travel, without any obstacles. This is one part of my life. Also part of my work. But there are other things too, because I am also a mother. And I am also a person, a personal person. And the single lesbians I know live their lives, and sometimes I would like to be like them, but I cannot.

Christina's Italian lover Patrizia thus sympathized with her sentiments, noting that although single women with children face similar problems, the situation for lesbian mothers within a lesbian culture is more difficult, as they are surrounded by independent women without children. Patrizia is now co-parenting Christina's ten-year-old son Philipp, after spending many years herself as a lesbian without children. She sees a fundamental difference between the two ways of life, remarking that being a lesbian with a child

> means more connection with reality. To not remain young, lesbian, intellectual, and to not remain a teenager. I know so many lesbians who are in their thirties; they live like teenagers, without any relationship with the reality of their age. It's possible to take responsibilities and to do a lot of things in political and social life. But I think it is important to live with another generation, and have responsibility towards the generation that is growing up – each age of life.

Christina and Patrizia recently took Philipp to a lesbian film festival in Italy, but, as a boy, he was not allowed inside the cinema. Christina had mixed feelings about her son's exclusion. She didn't question the lack of formal childcare at the festival itself: that the children would be looked after by friends or family was considered a fair assumption in Italy. Although barred from the cinema, Philipp was allowed into the café where meals were organized, but even this would not be possible had he been a little bit older. Now he is ten, Christina says, 'I feel he is at a borderline. Maybe in one year it will be quite different and I cannot bring him.'

In Italy, the strict rules and expectations about how women should live their lives come from society in general, rather than from within the lesbian community. In the north of Italy, the lesbian community is quite visible and active, organizing film festivals and Gay Pride, socializing, and lobbying for lesbian and gay rights, including rights for non-biological mothers. Motherhood is one of the issues addressed by the community: in the Italian lesbian week in May 1996, a seminar was held on lesbian motherhood. Children are accepted and generally welcomed as a normal part of this community. The pressure on women to marry and have children is so strong that many lesbians, especially older lesbians, have had a heterosexual past. Nowadays, with the increasing visibility of lesbians and gays presenting an alternative to compulsory heterosexuality, more and more lesbians are resisting these pressures. Mostly, however, they consider themselves lucky to have avoided heterosexuality, rather than condemning those who didn't. There seems to be a certain solidarity between mothers and non-mothers, perhaps because all lesbians in Italy have to deal with a lot of prejudice from society, regardless of whether they have children.

One lesbian couple who also have a ten-year-old son spend all their time with lesbians (they say they don't know any heterosexuals) and find that their friends welcome their boy with open arms. Meetings are held at their house when their son is with them, and persuading friends to play with him and keep him amused so they can take part in the meeting is not a problem. Although they appreciate all the attention given to their son by childless friends, contact with other lesbians with children, is especially important for their child. As his father is very involved in a Catholic organization, the boy spends a lot of time around families with traditional Catholic values, so he feels different from the other children around him simply because his mother and father have separated. Spending time playing with and talking to other children from lesbian families helps him to overcome this feeling of difference.

Lesbian mothers in the south of Italy have the hardest time, according to Bianca, who lives in the north but works for a telephone helpline for lesbians from all over Italy. She paints a grim picture: dependence, isolation and invisibility. Half of the calls she receives are from women who are married, usually with children: job opportunities for women in the south are almost non-existent, she explains, so women have little choice but to marry, otherwise they have to continue living with their parents. There is strong element of social control in their lives, as everyone around them knows precisely who they are, what they are doing, and who with. Breaking free can seem impossible, as only money can buy independence. A local lesbian community cannot thrive under such conditions, so Bianca believes that most end up having secret, unhappy affairs with married heterosexual women.

Bianca, now in her early forties, became a mother when she was twenty as an act of rebellion against the expectations placed upon her by her own mother, but this act quickly backfired.

> My coming out as a feminist occurred after the birth of my daughter, because being a mother immediately made me realize that I was no longer an individual. I was the mother of, and the wife of … I was no more Bianca. Bianca did not exist. And I could not accept this; I just could not accept this. So from this moment on, I made a lot of choices that in the end brought me to come out as a lesbian.

Although Bianca rejected the identity of mother, this did not mean that she rejected her daughter:

> I had to free myself and I had to free my daughter, because if I succeeded in freeing only myself, it would not have been a victory. I had to fight for both of us. And

that is why I decided to have my daughter with me and I fought to have the legal custody of her.

If Bianca could free herself completely of all society's pressures and do whatever she wanted, she would choose to live her life differently and not be a mother:

I know it's not very good. But it's the truth. And not being a mother, I could have done a lot of things that I could not do because I was a mother. For example, I would not have done ... a boring job in an office for seventeen years. I would have had the possibility of being myself much more often than I had. And I would have the possibility to decide things just for me. Because when you are a mother, you have to forget yourself. I mean, if you are lucky, you could be fifty-fifty, but when you have a child, all your life must take into account the fact that you have a child. So all choices are different.

Unsurprisingly, then, Bianca has little interest in meeting other lesbian mothers in her town:

I am myself before being a mother and I don't want to conceal myself behind my motherhood. This way of seeing things, it's an obstacle to having mother friends. My way of being a mother, of interacting with a child is really different from theirs. I think – the ones I knew – they are too traditional for me, and I can't stand it.

Bianca has always brought up her daughter in an unconventional way, seeking out ways to broaden her horizons even when she was very young by sending her to an alternative nursery school that experimented with anti-authoritarian and anti-sexist methods of teaching.

Bianca's rejection of convention and search for a way to live her life according to her own ideas and ideals has taken her outside Italy to an international community of radical lesbians. Here, the attitudes are reversed: instead of lesbians facing prejudice, it is the mothers who do not fit in. In these circles, children are not welcome, and lesbian mothers are invisible and unwilling to show themselves for fear of condemnation. Although she agrees with the anti-motherhood sentiment within the community, as a radical lesbian who has a child, Bianca would like to meet other mothers who face similar dilemmas.

It's not normal for a lesbian mother when she goes to groups to say she's a lesbian mother. Partly for fear, of course, because she doesn't trust even the lesbians. Or just because she thinks that she won't find anyone for the evening or for life. Lesbians, at least in my experience, don't like lesbian mothers. You are stigmatized as a traitor. You were wrong once, you were with the enemy. It's not very easy to be accepted. A lot of times I find myself asking the audience at meetings, where are the mothers? Come out! And no one says anything and afterwards in the corridors, talking privately, they say, you know, I'm a mother too. It's very difficult, very, very difficult.

These anti-motherhood views are articulated in no uncertain terms by one of Bianca's friends whom she met through radical lesbian meetings. Marian, a slight woman in her thirties with an intense gaze, has run the only lesbian bookshop in Brussels virtually single-handedly since 1986. She is well known in lesbian circles in Belgium and abroad for her commitment to lesbian activism and her strong opinions, including her opposition to lesbian motherhood. Marian agreed to be interviewed for this book as she says she laments the decline of political discussion about motherhood within the lesbian movement: 'Fifteen years ago, the lesbian movement was critical of the institution of motherhood, but today criticism is unwelcome.'

Marian is very resentful of what she sees as the over-importance given to motherhood believing that lesbian mothers are more tolerated and accepted by mainstream society than single lesbians: 'Lesbians who reject motherhood are accused of being antisocial and unfeeling. In the past, these accusations came from heterosexuals. Now they come from other lesbians as well.' She views motherhood as an institution imposed on women with the aim of perpetuating existing society rather than introducing new values. 'Lesbian mothers tend to reproduce marriage and the nuclear family,' Marian claims. 'Having responsibility for supporting their children means that lesbian mothers are obliged to compromise. They try to fit in with society rather than becoming visible and risk losing their jobs.' Marian sees nothing but disadvantages in having babies. When women decide to become mothers, their lives become restricted, she argues. Raising their children means that lesbians lack both time and money to engage in other activities, particularly within the lesbian community. In her opinion, lesbian mothers tend to be isolated and build their lives around their children, so their lesbian identity disappears into motherhood and they have no time for themselves.

Boys in the lesbian community is one subject that brings out all Marian's ire. Frustrated by what she sees as the power imbalance between lesbians and male children, who carry more weight in society, she is passionately in favour of providing women-only space where no men are allowed, not even children. Lesbians are trying to redress this balance, she explains, by giving priority to lesbians who want no contact at all with the male sex, and who won't feel able to come to an event if they are present, whatever their age: 'The aim of women-only space is to be open for all women, but by accepting boys, some lesbians are excluded.'

In Paris, also a hotbed of radical lesbians, one lesbian has found that having children makes romance problematic. Sylvie has come across mixed reactions to her motherhood during her activities in the more militant lesbian scene, ranging from sympathy to distrust and questioning about whether she is a real lesbian. She writes: 'Some envy me, others feel sorry for me (it's hard to bring up children on your own), some are afraid when I flirt with them, others wonder if, deep down, I'm not still a bit heterosexual (therefore bi) and are a bit suspicious …'

Suspicion of their latent heterosexuality has also been a problem for lesbian mothers in Greece: many of them have been married at some point in their lives, and other lesbians think of them as being able to be straight again if they so wish. As a result, mothers are usually isolated from the lesbian community there. Only one lesbian mother is involved in the lesbian caucus of the Greek Homosexual Community. She has four children, all girls. Public attitudes towards lesbians are so hostile that most lesbians are very closeted. Lesbian mothers face even greater condemnation: people believe that lesbians are unfit to be mothers because their 'sexual deviance' will turn their children into homosexuals too. When lesbians are forced to battle against such prejudice, it is not surprising that they erect defences, and form small, closed groups. In this situation, issues of trust within the community are all the more important: anyone perceived as able to cross the lines and return to the hostile outside world may be regarded with deep suspicion.

Fear can keep lesbians and mothers apart: in hostile environments, women may be afraid to be identified as lesbian mothers because of the very real danger they would face of losing their children, while lesbian organizations are lobbying simply for the right for lesbians to exist, rather than focusing on parenting issues.

In Serbia there is a great divide between women who identify as lesbians and those who identify as women-loving-women who have children. Out lesbian activist Lepa writes that of the few lesbian mothers she knows, none of them identify as lesbian, tell their children about their sexuality or bring their lover into the family as a co-mother. Being labelled as lesbian would open them up to the risk of losing their children, in a country where, in the eyes of judges, lesbians fall into the same category as drug addicts and the mentally ill. These women keep their distance from the lesbian activist group Labris, which has never organized any public events or campaigns about lesbian family issues, nor has it ever been asked to by lesbians who have children. Rather, Labris is focusing its work on the issue of lesbian rights as human rights. In Lepa's view the Serbian public is nowhere near ready to take on board the issue of lesbian and gay parenting rights: 'We are at point zero concerning the lesbian family.'

Fear of not being welcome or accepted by the lesbian community can also keep lesbian mothers away. One lesbian mother from the Czech Republic has a very negative perception of the lesbian community, and cannot imagine herself fitting in there. Apparently, this has more to do with her heterosexual past than her motherhood:

> When there are more of these homosexual women together, I feel out of place. My partner ... she feels there like a fish out of water. I don't think this is only due to the child, I think that the homosexual women differ from the heterosexual ones, they are simply different.

She feels she has nothing in common with other lesbians, that they come from a different world to the one she inhabits:

> They differ, because either they are, or they act, or pretend to be different, yet they are all highly emancipated, independent; they ... let you see that they are able to dispense with a man, even in a showy and unnatural way, and it irritates me. I don't know why, but it simply irritates me [laughs]. 'They have also different interests from mine and I cannot talk about typically women's issues with them, because they look at me in such a manner ... although they are women they somewhat look down on me, in a very unpleasant way.

Lack of confidence is a major factor in her fear:

> I was raised in such a manner that I would never dare to come out to society alone. I was scared of going among homosexual women alone. Even my partner has pushed me many times: go, I will look after the boy. No, it is not possible. What would I do there alone? I simply must have some company.

Ironically, it was on the one occasion that she did venture alone to a lesbian meeting, that she met her current lover: 'I am terribly happy that I have her, my partner, whom I met in the first meeting in the L-Club. It took great courage! To go there for the first time.'

Breaking down preconceptions of each other and building bridges between mothers and non-mothers in the Czech lesbian community is one of the aims of the lesbian weekends organized by the lesbian group, Promluv. Lesbian mothers and their children have the opportunity to spend time in the countryside outside Prague relaxing and enjoying themselves with other lesbian families. Space and time is also provided for discussion between lesbians who choose to have children and those who do not, helping promote mutual acceptance and understanding.

In Poland, Joanna is the first to bridge the gap between mothers and the lesbian and gay community. She has worked in the 'faggoty' community, as she describes it, for five years, but at the time of the interview in late 1994 had never met any lesbian mothers. During all those years, she has had only one letter about the issue: from a woman who was married but childless and whose girlfriend was married with two children. Lesbians in general are very closeted in Poland, often for fear of losing their jobs, and lesbian mothers remain invisible because of the risk of losing their children. Advertisements do appear in gay publications from married women looking for a girlfriend, but these are rare. By 1996, mothers had become more visible in the lesbian community, to the extent that a weekly phone helpline was set up under the auspices of the national lesbian and gay organization.

Being the only visible lesbian mother around has its advantages, however, as Joanna has received nothing but support for her parenthood. Already an established figure inside the lesbian and gay community by the time she became a mother, the question of her acceptance by the community never arose. When asked about her friends' reaction to her recent motherhood, she answered 'normal' in a tone of sharp surprise, as if to say how else would they react? Many of Joanna's gay friends want children themselves and enjoy looking after her child. The fact that she slept with a man once does not call into question her sexual orientation; her friends just joke that she is not very credible as a representative of the gay movement. In fact, despite having a small child, Joanna is still very active in the community, and has even been spotted pushing her pram at International Lesbian and Gay Association conferences.

In Bulgaria, it is lesbian mothers who have taken the initiative to build a lesbian community and develop a lesbian identity. The newly formed Marita Club is run by two energetic women, one of whom has an adult son. They are determined to let far-flung lesbians know that they are not alone. Using a post box address, they are writing to all the publications they can find, proposing friendship and exchanges of addresses, information, art and magazines, and at the same time acting as a resource for women within the country.

Finding their place again within the community can be difficult for lesbians who drifted away after having children or starting a relationship with a woman with children. It is not always easy for them to reintegrate later, when the children are older. In France, in the 1970s, Benedicte used to live with a group of other lesbians and gays, but when she had a child, 'I stopped everything; that brought me another lifestyle'. For years she and her lover Nathalie hardly went out: 'previously we didn't allow ourselves such liberties while our daughter was at home.' Now that Benedicte's daughter is in her early teens, old enough to stay at home on her own for an evening, she and Nathalie would like to meet other women who love women, and go to lesbian events and parties. When Benedicte's work brought them to Belgium, it took them a year to make contact with the lesbian community, and even then, making friends was still difficult. Lesbian clubs are easy to find, but persuading strangers to start up a conversation is not. 'When we go to a party, we don't see anyone we know,' Benedicte sighed. They read the French magazine Lesbia to keep up to date on what is going on, and agreed to be interviewed for this book mainly to make contact with other lesbians with children.

For Benedicte and Nathalie, bringing their daughter with them when they go out is not an option, as they prefer to check out the people they meet first before introducing them to her. After living a closeted life in Catholic-influenced France where attitudes toward lesbianism are not always particularly open and accepting, they want to make sure that no one says anything hurtful to their daughter.

Mothers across Europe generally have mixed feelings about taking their children with them when they go out into the lesbian scene. Often their reasons are the same as for any parent, gay or straight. Loud, smoky clubs full of drunk people dancing have never been particularly child-friendly establishments, while the desire for peace and quiet, and private adult conversation away from the children, is felt to be necessary by parents whatever their sexual orientation. There are some concerns that are specific to lesbian mothers, however. One lesbian mother from the UK said she wouldn't bring her son to 'a big mixed homosexual gathering, because some of my friends are quite "camp". I feel that if I am at a party I want to enjoy myself without worrying about what he's thinking.' A French lesbian stated quite adamantly that taking her children to gay bars or nightclubs was out of the question, 'so as not to influence their sexuality'. In contrast, Geneviève had a more relaxed attitude about her daughter's exposure to gay life in Paris. Although she didn't take her daughter out clubbing, she took her everywhere else, as did her brother who is also gay. At thirty-one, Geneviève's daughter feels quite at home in the gay scene: 'Now that she is grown up, she loves to hang out with my gay friends. They are very nice and they adore her.'

Not everyone is so welcoming, though. Monyek related the sad tale of her attempts in 1994, when EuroPride was celebrated in Amsterdam, to organize lesbian mothers to walk together in the parade. Advertising in lesbian bars and other places lesbian mothers were likely to visit, she suggested that to make it a fun and visible event they come in pink and orange colours, with prams and children's bikes covered in flags, and she made a banner for the group. The parade organizer placed the lesbian mothers behind a group of women from a lesbian bar who were doing exercises to music, but the women from the bar refused, saying they would rather stand between the men. 'So I didn't want to argue at that moment – all those mothers with their children – so I said let's stand somewhere else, but I had never felt such a hard reaction on us being mothers in a heterosexual world.' At EuroPride 1996 in Copenhagen, however, children were back on the agenda, as the organizers included a series of presentations and debates on the theme of 'Gay and Lesbian Families'.

Finding the right environment to get together is an important step towards welcoming children into the community. Persuading parents to take advantage of that environment is equally important. In Denmark, one lesbian mother wrote that taking children to the local lesbian and gay bar/cafe/disco is not taboo, but when the bar owners arranged a family evening, not many families came. Denmark has a well-established lesbian community, in which politics and parenting mix together. The national lesbian and gay organization LBL has a number of local branches and support groups across the country, including one for lesbian and gay parents and potential parents, while the issue of insemination for lesbians is high on the lobbying agenda.

One lesbian mother has distanced herself from the activist part of the community since she and her lover had their child:

> We are very much a family, and family comes first before fun, parties and political activities. A whole generation of lesbians have not had children, and have been very active in politics (and parties). We are another generation. We are families, we are not very political, and we dress different.

Although she and her lover have had few problems with being openly lesbian in Denmark, this lesbian mother still acknowledged the need for political action by lesbians and gays: 'I think that even though we have a lot of rights in Denmark, and are tolerated, we still have to keep fighting for the rights we have and the rights we haven't gained yet.' However, now that she has her three-year-old son, her priorities have changed. 'I have been active in LBL ... but have chosen my family to come first.'

In the past, mothers were not so welcome in certain Danish lesbian circles. One mother writes: 'I was very conscious about not bringing my children to more "militant" meetings in the 1970s and 1980s. I formed a group with other lesbian mothers and their daughters. We met regularly and spent two summer vacations together.' She was concerned that such occasions should form only part of her children's social activity, adding, 'I spent three years living with heterosexual people, in a collective from 1981 to 1984, and I always found it important that my children did not get too isolated in a lesbian sub-culture.' Another lesbian mother from Denmark turned to the gay men's scene in her search for a more positive and supportive environment for her son:

> Fifteen years ago I wished for a daughter but I got a son. I did not want him to listen to lesbians talking negatively about men, about his sex, so I stayed away from almost all lesbian meetings and started to attend a group of gay teachers, mostly men. I have always tried to give my sons a close relationship to some men I respected. I want them to like and respect their own sex as part of their personality.

Nowadays in Denmark, rather than being excluded from political activity, building new family forms and bringing up children in an alternative way is seen as a political activity in itself. As one lesbian mother put it, 'my son gets to grow up in a community where gender roles are being challenged. He gets to see diversity in many respects, learns tolerance and that anyone is allowed to choose their own lifestyle.'

Clare and Debbie in the UK feel that the mere fact of living as lesbian mothers is a political act which influences the society around them. As Clare says: 'Everyone we encounter in our lives is changed a little bit by knowing us and their attitudes are forced to be challenged, whether it's our families or other kids at school.' Although they are confident in their dual identities as lesbians and mothers, Clare and Debbie are aware of a slight imbalance. Since having their two sons, parenting has become their main focus, but this is not a change that they welcome wholeheartedly. 'We miss cultivating our lesbian side; it takes a back seat and seems a bit of a luxury sometimes – there isn't time for it,' Clare said regretfully. In the UK, and especially in big cities such as Manchester and London, there are large lesbian communities which organize social and cultural events, publications, support groups and lobbying groups. But as Debbie pointed out, childcare responsibilities mean that access to such a sustaining community is not easy:

I mean, it's not just going to the pub, it's actually about what you get from being in those environments and I think we're less and less involved in that. We get more from our friends with kids and lesbians with kids, but when we go to Gay Pride I think we realise we're missing out.

Clare and Debbie were among the first lesbians in their circle of friends to have children by insemination, which aroused a lot of curiosity and interest, especially when their elder son John was born eight years ago. Debbie describes how friends they hadn't seen for years would come to the house to see him:

It was almost like they were wondering was he going to have three heads or things like that … all these people who we vaguely knew from the scene, and didn't even know they knew where we lived, suddenly were ringing at the door.

Initially the couple faced negative reactions from some friends who thought that children were a complete diversion and waste of energy, while others were provoked into reflecting on whether they also wanted children. Clare and Debbie felt like pioneers, leading the way. Eight years on, there has been a baby boom in the lesbian community in the UK, and many of the childless lesbians they used to know now have children themselves: 'In the last five or six years, I don't feel like we've had any good or bad reaction from the lesbian community, because the lesbian community became the lesbians with children community.' Given their long experience, the couple are still viewed as gurus, experts in the field of lesbian motherhood, and are called upon to act as role models, imparting advice to the next generation of lesbian mothers. They still get strangers knocking on their door, although nowadays the physical aspects of lesbian motherhood are less of a mystery, and the focus is more on how to do the actual childraising and avoid the pitfalls. With the baby boom, lesbian mothers are taking on a more prominent role in the community, and many lesbian mother groups have sprung up across the UK, especially in larger cities. Manchester now has a monthly social event for lesbians and their children which, according to Clare and Debbie, provides a sense of community for the children, as well as a support network for the mothers. Occasions such as Gay Pride marches are also important and exciting for the children, helping them to feel part of a wider community. John and Kevin are great fans: 'They love it, they really enjoy that as a gay festival, and they see themselves as belonging in that somehow.'

The baby boom is just coming to Finland, but previously Kati found that children were an invisible part of the lesbian community:

> There are of course a lot of lesbian mothers in Finland, but I have always wondered where they hid all their children. Finnish lesbian communities form a kind of bachelor culture, and kids don't fit there. I have been one of the few moms who take their kids to meetings and to parties, even to Gay Pride. I have never gotten any negative response, though, for bringing my kids everywhere with me.
>
> One funny thing. My gay male friends do not see me if I meet them on the street with a child. They simply quickly recognize 'there is a straight woman with a kid' and don't even look at me until I give them a push and say 'hello!' Lesbians do see me on the streets, with and without children.

As yet there are no groups for lesbian mothers in Finland, and as a non-biological lesbian mother Kati has not met any other women in a similar situation to her own, so has had to seek out her own community of lesbian mothers elsewhere:

> My lesbian mothers' community is in cyberspace. My most important lesbian mothers' community is the lesbian moms' list on the Internet, run by Dorsie Hathaway. So I have contact with some three hundred to four hundred mostly North American lesbian mothers. This is the place where I have found the most interesting discussion, for example, about problems with teenagers, in general, and in relation to

teenage kids' problems with openly lesbian moms and the kids' right to be closeted about their moms' lesbianism, problems with school beginners, and so on. This
Internet community has given me so much strength, so much knowledge, so much
fun – I would be a different mom without this community, much more closeted and
much more frightened than I am now.

Kati may not have to sit at her computer screen to meet lesbian
mothers for much longer. The tide is turning in Finland: a lesbian family hit the front pages in early 1996, when a famous Swedish rock star
registered her partnership with her Finnish lover, a mother with two
children. This high-profile event gave impetus to lobbying for rights
over children to be included in the partnership act for lesbians and
gays, at the time being presented to Parliament. This may also give
other mothers within the lesbian community a higher profile, and perhaps lead to the setting up of lesbian mother groups for those, like
Kati, who feel isolated.

The picture across Europe for lesbian mothers varies. In some countries with a hostile socio-political environment, the lesbian community is a closed circle, fighting for its own existence. Mothers are on the
outside, isolated, not daring to identify as lesbian for fear of losing
their children. In other countries, lesbian mothers are gradually finding their place within the lesbian community, or building it up themselves, and are opening it out to welcome children. Lesbian mothers
are becoming more visible within the lesbian community, and parenting issues are moving up the agenda. Lesbians are lobbying for the
right to have children, by insemination or adoption, and for legal
recognition of both the biological and the non-biological bonds within
lesbian families. The idea of this book was greeted with enthusiasm by
lesbian mothers and non-mothers alike, interested in looking beyond
the borders to get a glimpse into the lives of lesbian mothers from
across the continent. And by contributing their stories to this book, lesbian mothers have taken a small step toward developing a sense of
community across Europe.

Part Two

████

Country Profiles

Albania

ANTONIA YOUNG

Compiled November,1995

Statistical overview

Source: *Albania: A Country Study*, edited by R. Zickel and W. R. Iwaskiw. Research completed April 1992. Published 1994 by the Federal Research Division, Library of Congress, Washington; Institute of Statistics, National Library.

Capital: Tirana
Population: 3.3 million. In 1988, 37% of the population
was under 15 years of age
Languages: Albanian, Greek
Ethnic groups: Greek, Macedonian, Vlach, Montenegrin and Serb
Religions: Muslim 70%, Orthodox 20%, Catholic 10% (approx
imate)
Marriages: 26,989 (1995))
Divorces: 2108 (1994): one marraige in forty
Births: 70,954 (1995)
Deaths: 5 per 1000
Infant mortality: 39 per 1000 live births
Life expectancy: 79 for women, 72 for men

General climate and indicators

Albania was the last country in Europe to be freed from Turkish dom-
ination (1912) and the last to demand a democratic government (1991).
It emerged from the strictest form of Communism in Europe, and the
longest dictatorial rule (under Enver Hoxha 1945–85). Albania is the
only country in Europe (with the possible exception of Bosnia) with a

Muslim majority. Sixty-five per cent of the population lives in rural areas. The normal family arrangement is for newlyweds to be given a room within the groom's parental home and to remain there indefinitely. A high percentage of Albanian marriages are arranged, most in the rural areas and without any consultation with the bride-to-be. In this patriarchal society, even if women knew their rights, they would not dare to claim them.

Until 1944, the illiteracy rate in Albania was 85 per cent, closer to 100 per cent for women. In the nominal equality of the sexes under Communism, women were encouraged to work in the factories and the fields. However, this did not change their situation at home, where they were still expected to do all the domestic work as well. It has come as a relief to many that they have returned to the home without the additional burden of full-time outside employment (which brought only marginal extra income). On the other hand, without the minimal health and social security benefits enjoyed under Communism and the price control of essentials (such as bread and particularly rent for living accommodation), there is now greater need than ever for women to bring in extra income.

Before 1991, there was no dating system among the youth of Albania; even now this is a very new concept (giving some kind of equality to the sexes) and is only carried into practice by a few Westernized townspeople. Most young women are closely chaperoned. Until 1991, no contraceptive advice was publicly available and abortion was illegal. Even now, in spite of very little information on, and availablity of, contraceptive devices, illegitimacy is rare. Mothers who are widowed have the company and protection of their husband's parental family.

Prior to the Second World World War, male homosexuality was known to be practised in rural areas. In a society where traditionally only men expected to enjoy sexual pleasure, lesbianism could not have been seen to serve any purpose. Under Communism homosexuality was strictly forbidden. Article 137 of the Albanian penal code (repealed only in 1995) refers to 'pederasty' (defined as sexual relations between males of any age) and could even refer to someone who admitted just having such tendencies. This was punishable by up to ten years 'deprivation of liberty'. Despite the repeal of the law (to accommodate human rights demands in order for Albania to become eligible to join the Council of Europe), there is still strong pressure to crack down on gays, hence the reluctance of the members of the gay and lesbian organization, Gay Albania Society, to identify themselves. There are reportedly one or maybe two Albanian lesbians among the group, but networking has been effectively obstructed.

Legislation

This is a period of transition and the introduction of an entirely new legal system has not yet been put into place. Many of the concepts are entirely new and it may take a while for their significance and need to be assessed.

The future

The newly emerging women's organizations and plans for shelters for battered women are beginning to attract urban women, but it will be a long time before any effects are felt in rural areas. The situation in the towns can only become more open in the future; however, this is obviously going to be a long-term process and meanwhile gays will face continued hostility in this male-dominated society.

Support groups

Shoqata Gay Albania (Gay Albania Society)
Kuti Postare
(PO BOX) 104
Tirana

Kozara Kati
Human Rights Documentation Center
Rr. Komt. Urani 17
Tirana
Tel/FAX: (42) 42630

Austria

BABARA FRÖLICH
Compiled March 1996

Statistical overview

Source: *CIRCA*

Capital: Vienna
Population: 8 million (1994)
Languages: 93% speak German
The rights of Slovene and Croat-speaking minorities are protected.
There are 22,000 Croat, 16,000 Slovene, 12,000 Hungarian speakers of
Austrian nationality. Other languages spoken include Turkish 1.5%,
Serbo-Croat 2%, Croat 0.8%, Slovene 0.4%, Hungarian 0.4%,
Czechoslovak 0.2%
Religions: Roman Catholic 78%, Evangelical 5%, Muslim 2%,
other 6.4%, non-religious 8.6%
Divorces: 16,282 (1990)
Births: 12 per 1000 (1993)
Deaths: 11 per 1000 (1993)
Infant mortality: 7 per 1000 (1992)
Life expectancy: 80.1 for women, 73.9 for men (1994)

General climate and indicators

As a deeply rooted Catholic country, all family structures which go
beyond the traditional ones face difficulties and discrimination.
Austria still has laws which are specifically aimed against homosexuals. Article 209 forbids consenting sexual intercourse between gay men

under the age of eighteen, and Articles 220 and 221 prohibit both the advertising of a homosexual lifestyle in any positive way and the formation of homosexual groups. Consequently, lesbian mothers, in particular, remain very much in the closet.

Some lesbian mothers may be out to their children, but that is as far as it goes. Indeed, one mother explicitly said that her two children, although supporting her lifestyle, asked her not to expose it to their friends at school for fear of being laughed at or teased. Lesbian mothers keep their lifestyles very private and mostly remain outside the lesbian community. One reason for this is the fear of public exposure and the possibility that they might lose their children. Another reason however, concerns the lesbian community itself. Many lesbians reject the thought of a lesbian with a child, because they are reminded too much of the myth of the 'family.'

So, lesbian mothers not only face prejudice for being a lesbian, they are also confronted with prejudice from their own community for being a mother.

Legislation

Although in recent years there has been a concerted movement within the lesbian and gay community to fight for registered partnerships, so far it has not succeeded. This means that a lesbian co-parent does not have any rights in relation to the child of her partner.

Insemination, adoption and fostering

In Austria there is no legal access for lesbians to AI or adoption. The only way for a lesbian to have her wish for a child realized (if she does not want to have sexual contact with a man) is AI carried out privately. But so far information and advice is difficult to come by. In one known example, a woman medical doctor, who therefore had the knowhow and access to the relevant infrastructure, managed to become pregnant through AI.

Child and family benefits, childcare

In Austrian society a lesbian mother is treated as a single mother by the social welfare authorities, and receives financial support accordingly. However, she has to endure extra surveillance by social workers. Fearing gossip from neighbours, which could be passed on to the social worker, many lesbian mothers keep a low profile and lesbian couples often choose not to live together.

Support groups

HOSI Vienna
Gentzgasse 83
A-1180 Vienna
Tel: 43 1 470 29 60

Belgium

CLAIRE TIJSBAERT

Compiled May 1995; updated February 1996

Statistical overview

Source: *CIRCA*

Capital: Brussels (Bruxelles in French, Brussel in Dutch)
Population: 10 million (1994)
Languages: Flemish, French, German
Number of speakers: Flemish is spoken in the northern half of Belgium by 57% of the population and French in the southern half by 42%. Brussels, where 9.7% of the population lives, is a bilingual but predominantly French city, while there is a small German-speaking community of 67,000 in the east
Ethnic groups: Flemish, Walloon, European Union countries, Maghreb
Religions: Roman Catholic 84%, Muslim 2.5%, Protestant 0.5%, Jewish 0.4%
Marriages: 6.5 per 1000
Divorces: 28.8 per 100 marriages
Births: 12.42 per 1000 (1993)
Deaths: 10.51 per 1000 (1993)
Infant mortality: 7.94 per 1000 births
Life expectancy: 81 for women, 75 for men (1994)
Single mothers/ households headed by women: 7%

General climate and indicators

Belgium is a Catholic country, where society has a conservative attitude towards lesbians. If they have children, lesbians may be told that they need a man to help in their upbringing, so that the children may develop their gender and sex roles in a 'normal' way. These attitudes are held by the Vlaams Blok, a political party which promotes the traditional family, where the mother stays at home, the father is boss, and the ideal is to have as many children as possible. It is also very racist and homophobic.

The press, radio and television are currently very interested in lesbian issues, but the message they put across is often distorted. Seeing lesbians as 'hot stuff', the media is only interested in high viewing rates and sensational news.

However, the climate is changing in Belgium, as people are apparently becoming more tolerant. Although the increasing visibility of lesbians can provoke hostility, it is ultimately leading to a more open society.

Legislation

In the eyes of the law, a lesbian mother is a mother without a husband, unless, of course, she is married. Since 1985, a child born to a lesbian mother is considered by the law to have no father, but is regarded as a full and legitimate member of the mother's family, with the same status as other legitimate children.

The mother, like all single parents, may be given advice by a family council, mostly concerning property. The family council need not be from her family of origin, she could choose her partner as *teeziend veepd* or supervising guardian.

A lesbian mother cannot, however, bestow any legal rights on her female partner. She can make a will stating that her partner should become the guardian or adopt her child if she, the mother, dies, but this is only a wish; it is not legally binding, and could be contested in court. If a lesbian couple splits up, there is no way for the non-biological mother to claim the right to visit the child, unlike a father.

There is another difficulty which causes much fear among lesbian mothers. In Belgium, anyone who believes that a child is in danger is allowed to report their fears to the comitee bijzondere jeugdzorg or childcare committee. Having a lesbian mother or living in a lesbian household could constitute a reason for making such a report. In most cases, there would be an investigation by social workers, which might lead to interference by the committee, a court case and the removal of the child. Thus, many lesbian mothers are forced to hide their situation even from their children. In some cases, children have been taken away for this reason, or women have had to swear that they were not lesbian.

It is also the case that custody arrangements made during the divorce can later be changed. In 1994, a lesbian won such a case. Her husband, who had a new girlfriend, asked the court that his ex-wife be prevented from co-parenting, citing her lesbianism as the reason. The judge, however, did not agree, arguing that the husband knew his wife was a lesbian when they made the original co-parenting arrangement.

Insemination, adoption and fostering

SI with sperm from a male friend is always possible. However, there is a problem concerning sexually transmitted diseases, as no labora - tory will agree to save the sperm for the three months that is required to establish that the donor is not HIV-positive.

Donor insemination may be practised by some individual GPs and gynaecologists without any questions asked, even if they are told the woman is a lesbian. The Care Centre of Family Planning (Centrum Seksuele Voorlichting) practises donor insemination, where the terms are the same for heterosexuals and lesbians. And lesbians are also referred to the university clinic at Jette in Brussels, or to the Erasmus hospital, although the latter is rather more restrictive. Since 1981, the Jette clinic's official policy has been that there should be no discrimination against single women or lesbian couples over access to AI . The counsellor there reports that since she started work, she has seen fifty-two Belgian lesbian couples and about thirty French couples.

In Belgium only married couples or single persons as individuals are able to adopt children. In the case of a lesbian couple, only one of them would be allowed to adopt, and no legal connection with the other partner would be possible. As most adoption organizations are Catholic, or give priority to the well-being of the child, they are likely to view the lesbianism of the woman wanting to adopt the child as an extra problem in an already difficult situation.

Lesbians wanting to foster children find themselves in a similar position to those who wish to adopt. It may be possible if the woman conceals her lesbianism, or if the organization decides not to ask questions about two women living together. Otherwise, they would inevitably face the same difficulties.

Child and family benefits, childcare

Child and family benefits are the same as for single mothers, the only difference being that if a woman is openly lesbian she will have to deal with the inevitable prejudices about lesbians and children. Official child care during the day in a creche is cheaper for lesbian couples with children than for heterosexual couples. When setting the fee, only the income of the biological mother will be included in the calculation, as the child has no legal link with her co-mother.

The future

Within the coming years, a non-discrimination Act may be voted into Belgian law.

In September 1995, the Federation of Working Groups on Homosexuality circulated a petition asking for support against discrimination, including discriminatory legislation, against homosexuals in general, which was signed by no fewer than 170 social and cultural organizations. It virtually constituted an unofficial survey on the positions taken on principle by these various groups. Of particular interest were the reactions from the political parties. The Socialists, the Greens, and the VU (People's Union – a progressive federalist Flemish party) have an official party policy on the equal treatment of homosexuals. The VU is the only political party in Flanders to have a homosexual group, called the Pink Lions (the lion is the symbol on the Flemish flag), and the Socialists and Greens were the first to submit anti-discrimination resolutions and projects for partner contracts. The Liberals claim that they are against any discrimination on the basis of sexual preference. The Catholics (CVP – Christian People's Party – social democrats) presented a working document stating: 'The discrimination in the field of social rights and obligations (social security, inheritance, legislation, fiscal legislation) must be removed. The CVP is completely willing to collaborate in this.'

The City of Antwerp officially opened a register from 1 January

1996, where people can register themselves as living together regardless of whether they are same-sex or hetrosexual couples. No legal rights are conferred by the registration, but the move has important symbolic significance in the historically conservative Flanders region. The cities of Ghent, Oostende and Mechelen are also considering similar proposals. The aim is to push the federal government to adopt a registered partnership law at national level. These laws will not include parenthood of same-sex partners, nor will they allow for adoption.

Support groups

via Centrum Seksuele Voorlichting (CSV)
Guinardstraat 34
9000 Ghent
Tel: 091 25 06 52

VUB University Clinic at Jette
Academisch Ziekenhuis Jette
Laarbeeklaan 101
1090 Jette
Tel: 02 629 2487

Federatie Werkgroepen Homosexualiteit (FWH)
Vlaanderenstraat 22
9000 Ghent
Tel: 09 223 69 29

Tels Quels
81 rue Marché au Charbon
1000 Brussels

Bulgaria

LISA A. MULHOLLAND

Compiled May 1996

Statistical overview

Sources: UNDP reports; *ILO Statistical Yearbook 1993*; *Women and Political Transitions in South America and Eastern and Central Europe: Prospects for Democracy* (International and Public Affairs Center, Occidental College, California); private letters

Capital: Sofia
Population: 8,800,000 (1994)
Languages: chiefly Bulgarian
Bulgarian 7,680,000; Turkish 770,000; Macedonian 230,000; Romany 230,000; Armenian 30,000; Russian 20,000; Other 50,000
Religions: Bulgarian Orthodox 85%, Muslim 10%, Jewish 0.8%
Divorces: 11,341 (1989)
Births: 10 per 1000 (1993)
Deaths: 13 per 1000 (1993)
Infant mortality: 16 per 1000 (1989)
Life expectancy: 74.8 for women, 67.8 for men (1994)

General climate and indicators

The overall situation for women in Bulgaria continues to be one of economic, social and political transition. In 1991, 12.9 per cent of parliamentary representatives were women. This number increased to 14.5 in 1995. Public visibility has not necessarily led to a strong position for women, however, as politicians take women's rights for granted, as already achieved under the old system, and for the most part do not act as special advocates for women's issues.

Various women's groups were already operating by 1991, but continue to fill basic needs in civil society without having long-term strategies. Women entrepreneurial groups tend to focus on cultural and charitable activities.

Women are well represented in professional fields and education yet continue to work more than 21 per cent longer hours than men. As in other central European countries, women are seen as having final responsiblity for the inevitable children, and the family home, as well as working in the labour market out of economic necessity.

A number of lesbians in Plovdiv have organised the Marita Club. There is no special section for lesbian mothers as only a few are known to the club. In searching for contacts both in and outside of the country they sent letters of introduction to European magazines and groups. The following is taken from that original letter:

Our country Bulgaria is a former Communist state. Democracy in it is too young and although we do not suffer any sever discimination, still there are many who are unsympathetic towards us and we are not well accepted by society.

Homosexual people are often considered of lower intelligence. Homosexuality is treated by many as a miserable disease of the mind. There is little tolerance, primarily from the younger generation. For these reasons, gay men and women are forced to conceal their sexual preferences and have little opportunity to contact each other.

We have a great desire to learn more about lesbian rights and to obtain an idea of how lesbians live, think and feel all over the world. We believe in lesbian friendship and solidarity.

Support group

MARITA Club
PO Box 50
Plovdiv 4000

Croatia

LISA A. MULHOLLAND
Compiled March 1996

Efforts to find a single profile writer for Croatia did not meet with success. Instead the following is compiled from information gathered from the *World Atlas 1995*; a conference report on Croatia written by Andrea Spehar and Amir Hanusic of Lesbian and Gay Men Action (LIGMA) for an ILGA conference in 1993; a report on the status of women in Croatia (1995) created and distributed via e-mail by Grupa za Zenska Ljudska Prava B.a.B.e.(Women's Human Rights Group); and an e-mail response from Djurdja Knezevic in February 1996.

Statistical overview

Sources: see above

Capital: Zagreb
Population: 4,500,000 (1994)
Languages: Croatian
Ethnic groups: Croats, Serbs, Hungarians, Slovenes, Czechs and Albanians
Religions: Roman Catholic 76.5%, Orthodox 11.7% , Muslim 1.2% (1991)
Infant mortality: 9 per 1000 (1994)
Life expectancy: 76.5 for women, 68.1 for men (1994)

General climate and indicators

Following the cessation of war, the entire region of former Yugoslavia is undergoing a significant period of transition.

Public sentiment is against homosexuality in general and there are no openly gay or lesbian clubs in Zagreb, a city of about one million inhabitants. Gay men face verbal and physical attack in the street. Lesbians remain mostly invisible, but are regarded as sick, dirty or mad, and the term is used as an insult. Single women are also not highly respected, reflecting the current push towards an increased birth rate. As a result of the prevailing anti-lesbian feeling, lesbian mothers keep themselves out of the public eye and have never had a publicized gathering. Many remain in heterosexual marrages. The Catholic Church continues to promote families based on heterosexual marriage.

Legislation

Single mothers do fairly well under current legislation, but with homosexuality seen as a sickness, lesbian mothers face losing their children if challenged in court by the father or ex-husband.

Insemination, adoption and fostering

The rights of lesbians to insemination, fostering and adoption are not protected in Croatia. Married heterosexual couples receive preferential treatment.

Child and family benefits, childcare

Ba.B.e. reports the existance of decent maternity provisions, including 365 days of full paid maternity leave, the first six months of which is available to mother only and the second to either heterosexual parent, together with the possibility of two years' unpaid maternity leave with the right to reclaim the same job position.

However, a more recent unofficial report had this to say: 'The situation is getting rapidly worse. Cutting of social care is enormous. [There is] no money for newborn babies, kindergartens became too expensive and they are closing, and medical care is no longer free.'

Both sources commented that such restrictions only serve the government's stated goal of increasing the birth rate by pushing women into roles as full-time homemakers and mothers. Decrees by Catholic figures support this return to more 'traditional ways' with anti-abortion campaigns and pronouncements about motherhood.

The future

Indicators point to a long and difficult struggle not only for lesbians but many other social, economic or ethnic minorities in a conservative, militarized society which values women for their biological reproductive abilities above all else.

Support group

B.a.B.e. BABE-ZG@Zamir-zg.ztn.apc.org

Czech Republic

DÁSĂ FRANČÍKOVÁ

Compiled May 1996

Statistical overview

Source: Czech Office of Statistics, 1991-96

Capital: Prague
Population: 10,408,000 (1993)
Languages: Czech
Ethnic groups: Czech (96%), Slovaks 3%, Gypsy 1% (1993)
Religions: Atheist 39.8%, Roman Catholic 39.2%, Protestant 4.6 % (1993)
Marriages: 42,789 (1996)
Divorces: 23,394 (1996)
Births: 14 per 1000 (1991)
Deaths: 11 per 1000 (1993)
Infant mortality: 9 per 1000 (1994)
Life expectancy: 77 for women, 69 for men (1991)
Mothers: 43% of all women (1995)
Single mothers/households headed by women: 11% (1995)

General climate and indicators

The current situation in the Czech Republic reflects both the conservative and more tolerant opinions of society. The traditional nuclear family is still considered to be the norm; single mothers, however, are accepted by most people, especially if they were victims of domestic violence. According to statistics published in various Czech newspapers, Czechs in general don't consider homosexuality to have any large impact on their own lives, and most of them, wouldn't object to lesbian couples raising children. Sixty per cent of the respondents agree with same-sex partnership legislation. Such answers, however, must be treated with caution. When it comes to real life, positive responses are easily contradicted.

Although there are a number of foundations working on behalf of single mothers, their expert staffs of doctors, psychiatrists, lawyers and social workers, etc. either ignore the issues of lesbian motherhood or directly reject the suggestion that the situation of single mothers has any connection with lesbian mothers. Even members of supposedly open-minded human rights organizations can surprise with their intolerance and homophobia.

Homosexuality in the Czech Republic is viewed only on the sexual level and there is no discrimination against gays and lesbians in this area. Social discrimination, on the other hand, still remains, and lesbians often face difficulties in this regard if they decide to come out.

Legislation

There are no laws that acknowledge and/or protect lesbian mothers, who usually fall into the category of single mothers. At the present time they cannot live in a legally recognized relationship with their female partners. The Association of Organizations of Gay Citizens (SOHO) has been trying to get same-sex partnerships written into the new family law. In spite of the well-supported petition, sent repeatedly to members of Parliament, the proposal was rejected in November 1995. According to SOHO leader Jiri Hromada, the organization is currently trying to introduce registered partnership again, this time under civil law. As it is now written, registered partnership would legitimize the relationships of gays and lesbians, while ensuring them some of the same rights as partners in a heterosexual marriage, for example the co-ownership of an apartment and rights to inheritance. Questions of foreign partners and children are not addressed. There has been no organized effort by lesbian groups to comment on either of these issues. In the Czech judicial tradition custody of children falls to the mother in 93 per cent of cases. There are, however, cases of lesbian mothers being denied custody for reasons of sexuality, but it is rare for sexual orientation to be given as a reason for divorce.

Insemination, adoption and fostering

The original regulations covering access to donor insemination, adoption and fostering fail to include provisions for single parents. The amendment to the law enables single mothers to apply for adoption and fostering, but married couples are given preference. Rules and regulations applied to the selection process are extremely strict and involve long-term psychological tests. Among other things, applicants need to prove financial stability and good moral/social standing. Information on how successful lesbians have actually been in adopting or fostering is unavailable. AI is currently available only to legally married applicants living in common households.

Child and family benefits, childcare

Legislation concerning child and family benefits is currently undergoing some major changes. At present a woman receives a state payment when she gives birth to a child. She continues to receive a parent's supplement, with the amount being dependent on the total income of the household throughout her four-year maternity leave. New legislation provides the same benefit for fathers who wish to stay at home while their legally married wives return to work. Additional state payments are made for each child attending school, up to the age of twenty-six (again the amount depends on household income). If a divorced mother wishes she can receive monthly payments from her ex-husband to cover the children's expenses. Every employed mother also has access to day care centrers protected by law, the availability and accessibility of which remains good.

The future

Monika Benešová, a prominent member of the Promluv group, held a public commitment ceremony with her partner in a room in the Old Town Hall in Prague (an adjacent room is used for heterosexual marriages) in the spring of 1995, hoping to draw attention to the unsolved issue of registered partnership. The group dedicated an issue of their magazine in the autumn of 1995 to the topic of lesbian motherhood, touching on an unexplored yet thought-provoking issue. Promluv also organizes annual events (*Apriles*) and a lesbian autumn weekend, which both offer opportunities for all groups to discuss issues and deal with problems. In scheduling events, especially during *Apriles*, which are also open to the heterosexual community, Promluv strives to create a dialogue between communities, thereby spreading information and overcoming intolerance and homophobia. The lesbian weekend is especially comfortable for lesbian mothers, who able to give their children a few days out in the country in the company of other children with similar family situations. Time and space is also provided for discussion between lesbians who choose not to have children and those who do. In the end it will have to be representatives from both groups who promote the social acceptance of lesbianism and the legitimacy of lesbian motherhood as alternatives to heterosexual lifestyles.

Support groups

Lesbian Klub Lamda Praha
c/o Alia Magazine
Dělnìcká 31
170 00 Praha 7

Promluv
c/o Monika Beneśová, Anna Haasová and Jana Štepánová
Klimentska 17
110 00 Praha 1
Tel: (422) 26 97 215

Denmark
INGE-LISE PAULSEN AND VIBEKE NISSEN
Complied March 1995; updated September 1995, February 1995

Statistical overview

Source: Bureau of Danish Statistics

Capital: Copenhagen
Population: 5,215,718 (1995)
Languages: Danish
Ethnic groups: It is against the law to register people's ethnic origin, but compared to most other European countries Danish society is extremely homogenous. This is reflected in the small number of foreign nationals living in Denmark: 189,014 foreign nationals, including 24,192 from the Nordic countries, 31,245 from the European Union and 56,824 from the rest of Europe (including 34,658 from Turkey)
Religions: More than 80% of the population are members of the Danish State Church (Lutheran). Catholics, Jews, Muslims and other religions make up a very small percentage.
Marriages: 6.1% per 1000 (1993)
Divorces: 2.5% per 1000 (1993)
Marital status: population 4,127,366 adults over eighteen
    single: 1,560,872 (including non-registered lesbian and gay couples)
    married: 2,190,222 (including fewer than 200 under eighteen)

Official figures are for registered partnerships since it was introduced in 1989. The figures are for couples, but are based on the number of individuals, which is how the Danish statistics count them. Foreign nationals are not included. (There are probably a number of mixed partnerships.)

Registered single-sex partnerships:
    male couples: 1989: 263, 1990: 331, 1991: 193, 1992: 177, 1993: 160, 1994: 148.
    female couples: 1989: 62, 1990: 117, 1991: 95, 1992: 89, 1993: 82, 1994: 104.
    total male/female: 1821 couples.
The figures for 1995 are not yet available, but it seems as if the number of women and men registering is becoming more even.
Divorces: 162 male, 102 female
Deaths: 161 male, 16 female

In international statistics Danish registered partners become 'single' in order to make the statistics compatible.
Couples living together: 188,024
(Living together is defined as two people over 18 and of opposite sex who have children together and live at the same address)
Couples cohabiting: 356,866
(Cohabiting is defined as two people over 18 and of opposite sex with an age difference of less than fifteen years and no other adults at the same address; they may have children with other people)

Births: 1993   67,369,
1994   69,691 (preliminary, shows a growing tendency)
Deaths: 13.0 per 1000 (1994)
Infant mortality: 5.4 per 1000
Life expectancy: 77.76 for women, 72.49 for men (1992-93)
Mothers: Women born in 1950: at the age of 40, 91.8% have given birth to at least one child which survived for at least one year.
Households with child (ren) under 18 and only one adult (1994)
    single mothers: 104,500
    single fathers: 15,035
Children born outside formal marriage 46.8% (of total number of births (1994))

General climate and indicators

Danish society has changed dramatically since the 1960s and so, to a certain degree, have public attitudes. With easily available birth control and abortion, a divorce rate of 25 per cent and a percentage of women in the labour force almost equalling that of men, the word 'family' has taken on many meanings, and 'illegitimate children' no longer exist. Furthermore, the introduction in 1989 of the Law of Registered Partnership and subsequent media debates about lesbian mothers, insemination, adoption rights and church weddings for lesbians and gays have made homosexuality, and lesbian and gay families, quite visible.

It is never easy to be a single mother, whether lesbian or hetero - sexual; but it is probably less stigmatizing to be a single mother in Denmark, where almost half of all children are born to unmarried mothers, than in most other European countries. Lesbian motherhood certainly carries an additional stigma, but the most widely repeated argument against lesbian mothers is identical to the one used against other single mothers, namely, that 'a child needs a father'. Currently this argument is used frequently in the media as a way of explaining youth crime and other problems affecting young people.

Legislation

Due to social changes, Danish legislation is now focusing upon individuals rather than families. Thus a married couple is looked upon as two individuals rather than as one unit. The 'head of the family' has ceased to exist as an official concept, and although the average man still earns more than the average woman, there is no connection between a person's income and his or her married state.

Most of the laws concerning equal rights were passed during the 1970s, after Denmark entered the European Union. A crucial factor is that virtually all Danish women born after the Second World War are in the labour market (including unemployed women who are members of a union, and most people are union members). At the moment, more young women than young men are receiving a secondary education.

Thus, from a legal point of view, men and women have become

more equal, but the introduction of the law of registered partnership made it clear that although there are no Danish laws against 'promoting' homosexuality, lesbians and gay men are still not accepted on an equal footing with heterosexuals. The law of registered partnership gives lesbian and gay couples equal rights in terms of inheritance, insurance and pensions, but the right to adopt and to receive a blessing in a state church are excluded from the law. The exclusion of adoption rights may in part explain why only one-third of the approximately three thousand people who have chosen to register their partnerships are women.

A bill for shared parental rights recently received a lot of coverage before being passed, but in the end did not change much. The previous law had given people the right to choose between various alternatives in terms of legal parenthood. With the new law, married couples are granted shared parenthood automatically. Unmarried heterosexual couples living together have to apply for it, as do heterosexual couples who are not living together.

During the debate on shared parenthood, differences of opinion emerged between the various Danish women's organisations. Some wanted a new law, because they believed it would strengthen the rights and duties of fathers. But most organizations agreed that a choice of different possibilities is in the interest of the child and the mother. The importance of more and better counselling was also stressed and it was suggested that a study to be carried out on how the present system works before Parliament introduces a new system.

Insemination, adoption and fostering

Fostering is legally possible, as lesbians and gays are not specifically referred to or prohibited. But there are no available statistics, and in fact fostering is a non-issue in Denmark. However, lesbians are not allowed to adopt children, including those of their partners.

The exclusion of adoption rights from the law of registered partnership clearly discriminates against lesbian couples and their children. This was largely due to the political constellation in the Danish Parliament, but the situation may improve now that the Christian Party are no longer represented. It also probably reflects heterosexual fears about allowing gay men to adopt young children. There is a need for an information campaign to convince the public and the politicians that lesbians and gays ought to be able to adopt their partner's child.

In 1995, a preliminary report was published by the Ethical Council, an independent group of people whose job it is to make proposals to the government on difficult ethical questions. In 1989, a majority of the members of the Council were in favour of insemination for single women and lesbians, but in 1995, a small majority (9 vs. 8) were against it. In protest against this, the president (a gay man) and vice-president (a lesbian) of the national Danish lesbian and gay organization LBL, decided to arrange a 'marriage against discrimination'. So in September 1995, they got legally married at the Copenhagen Town Hall, and invited all the media. The marriage was designed to show the world that the registered partnership does not give the same rights as a heterosexual marriage in terms of insemination, adoption and church weddings. Not only did the event have great entertainment and publicity value but it also prompted one of the members of the Ethical Council to change her mind, resulting in a majority in favour of lesbian insemination.

Up to 1996, donor insemination of lesbians was not mentioned in any law, so in practice it has been left to the decision of individual doctors. Previously, LBL maintained a low profile over this, for fear that the laws might be changed for the worse. However, 1996 will see new national legislation on insemination for lesbians, and at the time of writing, the issue is under discussion at local government level. At a meeting held to discuss priorities in terms of economies in the public health sector, the only cutbacks to be authorized were insemination for lesbians, and circumcision. The savings here would have been negligible, as both these areas involve few people and have very low running costs. Moreover, at the same time, new areas were added, with the result that the new budgets are now higher than the previous ones.

Few lesbians have been inseminated in public hospitals, although some may have presented themselves and a gay friend as a heterosexual couple. Other lesbians have chosen insemination in one of the few private hospitals, where they are prepared to inseminate lesbians, but it is quite costly. A few gynaecologists offer insemination, which also costs money, but is not as expensive. There are no figures available for the total number of lesbians who have been inseminated.

Thus in practice lesbians do have access to donor insemination.

However, lesbians (single or in couples) who have children today seem to prefer SI using sperm donated by a gay friend, who then functions as a father on a personal and perhaps also on a legal basis.

Child and family benefits, childcare

In Denmark, all child and family benefits are administered by the authorities. If a mother decides to withhold the name of the father of her child, this has no effect on the child benefits she is entitled to receive. If, however, a lesbian mother and her partner live together on a permanent basis, or if they decide to register their partnership, the authorities may decide to cut down on social benefits. In other words, a lesbian cannot adopt her partner's child, but if she lives with the child's mother, she is expected to provide for that child. This is most certainly another major reason why only one-third of the couples who become registered partners are women.

The quality of public childcare in Denmark is high, and as range of facilities is quite extensive, nearly all Danish children spend a lot of time in public institutions. The system as such does not discriminate against lesbian mothers, but prejudice and ignorance on an individual level can make it quite hard for lesbians and their children to cope.

The future

As we say in Denmark, 'It is hard to make predictions, especially about the future'. However, it certainly looks as if lesbian mothers and their children will be able to live better lives in the future. Family forms, and norms, are changing rapidly. Everything is possible, and girls grow up with the knowledge that they will have to be able to take care of themselves. Also, sexual norms are changing, and young people leave home to live on their own at a very early age, compared, for example, to Spain. All this makes it easier to be different; in fact it is difficult to say what is 'normal'.

In this connection it is important to remember that Denmark is an extremely secular country. Church and state are separate entities, there are very few religious schools, and the Christian Party hasn't been able to muster two per cent of the vote, which would entitle them to four seats in Parliament.

Some new family structures are also emerging: for instance, lesbian couples and gay couples who create a family, have children together and share the responsibility. Sometimes the biological parents are legal parents, sometimes there is no legal father. A few years ago most lesbians favoured anonymous donors. Now the majority seem to want their child to have some kind of father. The most dramatic change has taken place among gay men, who are now beginning to think of themselves more and more as potential fathers.

Meanwhile, a number of problems remain unresolved. It seems likely that the adoption issue will not be solved for years to come. However, LBL are pushing for change. At the moment, the focus is on the Church, and as a result of LBL pressure, Danish bishops have just set up a working group whose task it is to discuss the issue of 'homosexuality and the church'. It is by no means unlikely that the outcome will be some kind of formal wedding ceremony for gays and lesbians.

Denmark is often looked upon as a lesbian and gay paradise. It is certainly true that as countries go, Denmark is a good country to live in for homosexuals. However, it is no paradise. Legally, and in terms of public opinion, we have come a long way, but we have our share of bigots, homophobes and sexists, and although much has been achieved, the never-ending task of consciousness-raising still remains.

Support groups

Lesbians and gays in Denmark organize in a number of ways, both separately and together. On a national level the largest group is the LBL, the National Association of Gays and Lesbians, which was formed in 1948. LBL has a number of local branches. Most of the work happens in groups - support groups, counselling groups, youth groups and women's groups. In Copenhagen, potential lesbian and gay parents have formed a group called *Forëldrespirer* (parentsprouts). The LBL national secretariat can be contacted at:

Knabrostrëde 3
Box 1023
DK-1007
Copenhagen K
Tel: 45 33 13 19 48
Fax: 45 33 91 03 48

Another useful contact is Kvindejuset (the Women's House) in
Copenhagen, which organizes feminist summer camps and courses
with childcare facilities: Their address is

Gothersgade 37
DK-1123
Copenhagen K
Tel: 45 33 14 28 04

Estonia
LILIAN KOTTER
Compiled February 1996

Statistical overview

Source: *CIRCA*

Capital: Tallinn
Population: 1,500,000 (1994)
Language: Estonian. New laws demand a knowledge of Estonian by the country's large Russian minority (30.3%), while Estonians are reluctant to use Russian.
Religions: Christianity is the dominant religion. The Evangelical Lutheran Church is the leading denomination; the Russian Orthodox Church is also represented.
Divorces: 5,785 (1990)
Births: 11 per 1000 (1993)
Deaths: 13 per 1000 (1993)
Life expectancy: 74.8 for women, 63.8 for men (1994)
Infant mortality: 13 per 1000 (1992)

General climate and indicators

There is no evidence of any well-known lesbians or lesbian groups in Estonia before the Second World War. Neither female nor male homosexuality was punishable; the article on male sodomy was introduced to Estonia directly from the Penal Code of the Russian Federation immediately after Soviet occupation in 1940. This did not mean, however, that lesbians were in a more favourable situation than gay men. Nobody, including heterosexuals, was able to live their private life freely. All kinds of spontaneous organizing were repressed by the

KGB, which had a higher standing than the law and the Communist Party itself. Sexual liberation, even straight sexuality, was regarded as something which promoted individuality and was thus considered to be dangerous for a totalitarian society.

Now that the harassment and ideological pressure has ended, those who suffered in the past can finally feel free, and possibly even more liberated than the rest of the population. This mental liberation has played its role in the relative success of Estonia's lesbian and gay movement since 1991. On the other hand, the present economic difficulties faced by the country, which is making the huge step from totalitarianism to a market economy and civil society, have been keeping the nation busy with more 'vital' problems than homosexuality.

At the end of the 1980s, thanks to glasnost, the silence around questions of sexuality and homosexuality was broken, and women identifying as lesbians were able to change their lives. The realization of the existence of homosexuality and homosexuals, however invisible, moved public attitudes toward tolerance. People are able to understand the needs of homosexuals, as they are quite similar to those of many Estonians during the years of national suppression.

Compared to the other Baltic states, Latvia and Lithuania, Estonian sexual minorities apparently bask in an atmosphere of tolerance. Most materials published during the first five or six years of the 1990s regard homosexuality positively; and the few, really exceptional homophobic attacks are usually followed by protest. The people seem to exercise a kind of inner censorship when it comes to expressing their views in public, and exhibit a reluctance (perhaps characteristic of small nations) to treat their minorities as outcasts, particularly such a large minority as homosexuals.

In the 1980s, the first gay and lesbian announcements began to appear in independent newspapers. In 1990, one of these led to the formation of a small group of women who drew up a strategy for further actions. In May 1990, a conference 'Sexual Minorities and Society in Twentieth-Century Europe', (the first of its kind in Eastern Europe), was held in the Estonian capital Tallinn. This represented a breakthrough in public opinion, as well as in the consciousness of lesbians and gays themselves, as the conference and its subject received positive press coverage. At the conference farewell party a group of

Estonian lesbians met with lesbians from Finland, the first time they had come into contact with lesbians from another country. A journalist commented that the meeting should be described as the First Congress of the Estonian Lesbian Union (ELU), and the name stuck.

The ELU was the first homosexual organization to be formed in the Baltic States, formally declaring its foundation on 13 October 1990. The event was covered by interviews with the ELU chairwoman in an independent newspaper and at peak viewing time on Estonian television.

The activities of the ELU include an information bulletin, a regular helpline, parties, fundraising events and sports activities. It also has a library, and young activists have compiled a book of interviews with lesbians. The ELU has been a member of the International Lesbian and Gay Association (ILGA) since 1991, and has attended several conferences. It is one of the partners in the ILGA Phare/Tacis Lesbian and Gay Anti-Discrimination project.

Transgendered people in Estonia often contact the ELU and take part in its events. Indeed, ELU serves as a kind of communication centre for transsexuals, who feel at home there. Most of the women associated with the ELU define themselves as lesbian, a few as bisexual. The majority are single, some are divorced and some still married. Since the end of the last century, the number of single women in Estonia has always been remarkably high, so compulsory marriage does not exist.

Several of the lesbians involved in the ELU have children, but lesbian mothers have not come to public attention or received media coverage in Estonia.

Legislation

Traditionally in Estonia, custody of children is usually awarded to the mother, unless she is considered asocial, for example if she is an alcoholic.

In a divorce case held in the Tallinn court in 1993, the husband demanded custody of his two children because his wife was a lesbian and lived with another woman. The lawyer objected, claiming that since the law does not mention lesbians there was no justifiable reason to refuse the woman custody of her children. As a result, the two women live together raising the two children. Lesbian relationships have no legal status in Estonia.

Insemination, adoption and fostering

Donor insemination is possible for a single woman in state clinics if she does not have medical counterindications. Although adoption and fostering is not easy because of long waiting lists, it is possible for a single woman to adopt a child, as long as she has a regular income and is able to provide a child with all it needs. A single lesbian wanting to adopt, however, would be advised not to reveal her lesbianism.

Child and family benefits, childcare

There is little financial support for single mothers, including lesbian mothers. Fathers are meant to pay 25 per cent of their income as maintenance per child automatically, but the problem of avoidance is quite widespread. The state pays a minimal amount of child benefit, and there is a general lack of childcare resources.

The future

Hopes for the future of lesbians and lesbian mothers in Estonia are summed up in the aims of the ELU:

1. to unite lesbians and bisexual women living in Estonia and to promote their self-awareness;
2. to arrange the exchange of information among lesbian and bisexual women in Estonia;
3. to provide normal and full-value living conditions in society for lesbians and bisexual women;
4. to protect the rights and interests of sexual minorities fighting against discrimination in society based on sexual bias;
5. to promote contacts with similar organizations in other countries;
6. to co-operate with legal experts in order to achieve the right of legal registration of marriages between lesbians and to work out legislation on adoption for lesbian couples;

7. to collaborate with other women's movements in Estonia and abroad;

8. to collaborate with gay and transsexual movements in Estonia and abroad.

Support group

Estonian Lesbian Union
Pk. 3245
EE0090 Tallinn
Estonia
Tel: (372 2) 449 743
Fax: (372 2) 216 205
e-mail: eluell@saturn.zzz.ee

Finland

KATI MUSTOLA AND PAULA KUOSMANEN

Compiled February 1996

Statistical overview

Source: *Statistical Yearbook of Finland 1994*

Capital: Helsinki

Population: 5,100,000 (1994)

Languages: Finnish 93.1%, Swedish 5.82%, Lapp 0.03%, Romany (1993)

Ethnic groups: Finnish, Saami (Lapp), Romany

Religions: Evangelical Lutheran (official), 86.5%, Finnish Orthodox 1.1%, Roman Catholic 0.7%.

Marriages: 9.5 per 1000 (1993)

Divorces: 14,365 (1989)

Births: 13 per 1000 (1993)

Deaths: 10 per 1000 (1993)

Infant mortality: 6 per 1000 (1992)

Life expectancy: 80.2 for women, 72.7 for men (1994)

Finnish family types (1993):

    married couple with children: 44.1%

    unmarried couple with children: 5.8%

    mother with children: 11.2%

    father with children: 1.9%

    married couple without children: 27.6%

    unmarried couple without children: 9.4%

Lesbian mothers

We have no recent research results on the number of lesbian mothers in Finland, but we have some information from a questionnaire-survey among the gay, lesbian and bisexual population from 1982. The sample is by no means representative (it is hardly possible to get a representative one) but it is very large: we received 1,051 answers, of which 323 (31%) were from women.

Of these 323 lesbian and bisexual women, 13% had children (10% of men had children). Of these children, 60% lived with their mothers (28 % of the children of gay/bisexual fathers lived with their fathers). Of all the people who answered the questionnaire, 30% of the women and 37 % of the men felt the desire to have a child. Probably the situation has changed during the last 14 years since this survey was conducted. (Source: Gronfors, M. and Haavio-Mannila, E. and Mustola, K. and Stalstrom, O.: Esitietoja homo-ja biseksuaalisten ihmisten elamantavasta ja syrjinnasta. In: Sievers, K. and Stalstrom, O.: *Rakkauden monet kasvot.* Espoo 1984. (Available only in Finnish))

General climate and indicators

Sexual acts between consenting same-sex adults, both male and female, were forbidden under Finnish law until 1971. The law criminalizing homosexual acts was in practice through the 1960s, and women were also convicted. Against this background, development in Finland has been rapid: from the decriminalization of same-sex sexual acts in 1971, to abolishing the categorization of homosexuality as a mental illness in 1981, to a law prohibiting discrimination on the basis of sexual orientation in 1995. A bill of registered partnership is also currently under discussion in 1996. Since Eva Dahlgren, a famous Swedish rock star who is also very popular in Finland, registered her partnership with her lover Efva Attling in January 1996, the debate on law reform has been heated in Finland.

Until the 1990s, homosexuality in general and lesbianism in particular were effectively invisible in the Finnish culture. Because of this invisibility there was no particular hatred or dismissal of lesbians; anti-gay attitudes were more directed towards gay men because the straight majority was more familiar with their public image. With the help of the very public coming-out of Eva Dahlgren and several well-known Finnish people, the situation is changing dramatically at the time of writing. But there is still a long way to go before any general under-standing and acceptance of lesbian motherhood is achieved.

Socially and symbolically lesbian mothers do not exist in Finnish culture. As a unified social identity, it is impossible to connect lesbian-ism and motherhood in the heads of most people, both straight and gay. Lesbian motherhood is seen as a taboo. Lesbian mothers are con-sidered as single mothers, both in straight culture and gay communi-ties. Lesbian co-mothers are the most non-existent mothers, especially if they are separated from their former lovers with whom they have had children. Even in lesbian communities, that a lesbian co-mother is a parent, and that the parenthood continues after the breakup of a les-bian relationship, is seen as an impossibility. There has been no public discussion about lesbian motherhood in the straight media and very little in lesbian publications. Lesbian biological mothers, of whom the majority have conceived their children in previous marriages or other straight relationships, remain invisible even in the lesbian communi-ties. Single motherhood on the other hand is nowadays quite well accepted in Finland, certainly in comparison with the 1950s, when sin-gle motherhood was seen as social failure and mark of a woman's bad reputation.

In Finland and in other Nordic countries, the model of the nuclear family differs from the American and central and western European model. The figure of the male breadwinner is very weak in Nordic countries, because in most families both parents work outside the home. In 1993 in Finland, 73 per cent of mothers with children under seven years of age were working, and the percentage of working mothers with children younger than three is 56 per cent. In the 1980s, the percentage of working mothers with small children in Finland used to be the highest in western Europe, and even higher than in many eastern European socialist countries; only the GDR had a high-er percentage. Part-time jobs for women are not and never have been popular in Finland, so most Finnish mothers work full time. This is very different to Sweden and some other countries, where many working mothers with small children are able to have part-time jobs.

This does not mean that motherhood is not an important part of womanhood in Finnish culture. But in everyday life, the ideal of the nuclear family has partly broken down. Statistically, only half of all Finnish families consist of two parents of different sexes and their children. Stepfamilies form an estimated 15 per cent of all families. Both female- and male-headed single families exist and are quite well accepted. Same-sex cohabiting couples are not counted as a family unit by the Central Office of Finnish Statistics, but to constitute one household for some welfare benefits.

Legislation

Lesbian relationships have no legal status in Finland. The Finnish lesbian and gay organization SETA is campaigning for legalized gay and lesbian partnerships. The proposal for a bill of registered partners, represented the most radical of all Nordic same-sex partnership bills because it included the right for a lesbian or gay co-parent to adopt the biological child of the partner, and for the couple to adopt a child together. This bill was proposed not by the government but by a number of progressive MPs, but fell through automatically in the wake of the new elections. At the time of writing, SETA is campaigning for a new bill which will also include the right to adopt. SETA has agreed upon the phrase 'recognized companionship' or 'legalized spouses' rather than 'registered partnership', the term used in other Nordic countries, as it may give the impression that homosexuals are listed in registers. 'Gay marriage' is the term mostly used by the media.

We have no information about custody cases where the mother's lesbianism has been an open issue, but probably there are such cases. Disclosure of the mother's lesbianism has been used successfully by the husband to exert pressure in many custody cases. Usually the custody of the children is given to the mother unless there is some doubt about the mother's ability to take care of the children, for example because of alcoholism. In some of the cases known to us, custody of the children has been given to the father after he threatened to disclose the mother's lesbianism and the mother had to agree.

Conceiving children by AI is so new to Finland that details about custody cases or other problems are not available. Because there is no partnership legislation or shared lesbian adoption, the lesbian co-mother has no official right to make custody of the children an issue in the court or the welfare office.

Insemination, adoption and fostering

No legislation that would expressly deny lesbians their right to par-take of donor insemination currently exists in Finland. Nevertheless the Finnish Medical Association has issued guidelines to its members advising them not to inseminate single women, which interestingly includes the category of lesbian women. These guidelines are, how - ever, not binding. The decision to perform an insemination is taken individually by each doctor. While some doctors fear damage to their reputation, others see it as their professional responsibility to help their patients, rather than leaving them to use untested semen.

Since 1982, different Finnish working groups set up by the National Board of Health and the Ministry of Justice have been preparing pro-posals for legislation on artificial procreation. The 1991 proposal by the Ministry of Justice suggested restricting its use specifically to heterosexual couples who are married or live in a relationship similar to marriage. The reasoning behind this proposal was to ensure a balanced life for the prospective child (something which according to the proposal is not possible if the child is born without a father). The proposal has still to reach the final decision-making bodies, and is currently being circulated for further comments. At the time of writing, the latest information on this issue suggests that changes have been made to the proposal, which will offer better prospects for women who find themselves outside the conventional nuclear family. (Source: Maria Hynna, 'Alternative Insemination of Lesbian Women'. Essay for the course *The Gender System in Nordic Countries*, Abo Akademi, 1995).

If a lesbian presents herself to the authorities as a single person (the authorities assume her to be a single heterosexual woman, unless advised otherwise) she may be eligible to adopt or foster a child. Usually single parents get an older or handicapped child. If the person works in the educational or social sector, she or he is seen as a good potential parent or foster parent.

Child and family benefits, childcare

Lesbian mothers and even stepfamilies headed by lesbians are treated as single-mother families and receive all the same social benefits as

straight single mothers. Since 1 January 1996 every child in Finland
has had a right to free or low cost communal childcare. It is very common in Finland to use communal childcare facilities, and the children
of lesbian mothers are no exception to this.

The future

The lesbian baby boom has only just arrived in Finland, and many lesbians and lesbian couples are considering conceiving a baby in the
near future. As far as we know, two to three children have been born
by SI in Finland, and some women have sought help from medical
doctors with AI treatment (via a sperm bank) or with fertility problems. In both cases known to us, the doctors in question were very
positive and willing to help, but for different reasons there were no
successful pregnancies. But there may be many more successful cases
about which we have no information.

There have been two or three articles in gay magazines on lesbian
motherhood, and a couple of articles in women's magazines on motherhood in which lesbian mothers have also been interviewed. Finnish
television has screened two foreign documentaries – one British and
one Danish – on lesbian motherhood. Finnish lesbian mothers in general, however, are reluctant to present themselves in the media as lesbian mothers, as they are afraid of their children being harassed. Since
the 'marriage' of Eva Dahlgren, however, as the media calls her partnership, gay and lesbian relationships have attracted particular media
interest. In February 1996, two Finnish lesbian mothers were interviewed on television, and in the first week of March, three hundred
articles mentioning homosexuality appeared in the Finnish media.

The whole circus surrounding Eva Dahlgren's 'marriage' shows
how important it is to have positive role models: one hundred 'ordinary' lesbians would never attract as much public attention as one
famous one. Efva Attling, Eva Dahlgren's spouse, has two sons from a
former marriage aged four and eight. Now suddenly we have a
prominent two-mother-lesbian family on the front pages and prime-
time news. Their 'wedding' was a huge media event in Sweden, too,
and their older son was subsequently harassed at his school. The
school immediately called a crisis meeting, where teachers, pupils and
both mothers tried to solve the problem. This event failed to make the

news in Finland, which is symptomatic of the Finnish situation: although the media is eager to discuss lesbian and gay partnerships, it is not ready to move on to lesbian and gay parenting.

Support groups

In the 1980s, there was a lesbian-feminist group called AKANAT, which also focused on the issue of lesbian motherhood. In the 1990s, several groups have organized around specific issues: lesbian homes for the aged (MUMMOLAAKSO), lesbian studies networks, lesbian sports groups, lesbian glamour parties, etc., but , interestingly, there is not yet a group for lesbian mothers.

The contact address for the mixed gay and lesbian organization is:
SETA
PO Box 55
FIN-00531
Helsinki

France

AUDREY VAN TUYCKOM AND MICHELE DE DOBBELEER

Compiled March 1996

Statistical overview

Source: *CIRCA*

Capital: Paris

Population: 58,000,000 (1994)

Languages: French 53,200,000; Arabic 1,500,000; German and related dialects 1,200,000; Breton 900,000; Catalan 300,000; Italian/Corsican 200,000; Flemish 200,000; Basque 150,000

Main religions: Roman Catholic 76.3%, Muslim 4.5%, Protestant 1.4%, Jewish 1.3%, others and unaffiliated 13%.

Divorces: 105,813 (1990)

Births: 13 per 1000 (1993)

Deaths: 10 per 1000 (1993)

Life expectancy: 81.3 for women, 73.8 for men (1994)

Infant mortality: 7 per 1000 (1992)

Single mothers/households headed by women: 1,200,000 (1994)

General climate and indicators

The French climate is very strict, with the right wing in power since the general elections in 1993 and a rightwing president in power since 1995. The culture is strongly influenced by religion, despite being secular according to the constitution. Women are generally under-represented in political life. The political picture is not all gloom, however, as some politicians have acknowledged that the current laws do not take into consideration the needs of members of the different family structures that exist in France.

Not many lesbians are publicly out, only those pioneers, people who can 'afford' to be out for various reasons. There is a wish for visibility in the lesbian and gay community, and a desire to break the silence and taboos which exist even in Paris, and which are suffocating in the provinces. Attendance at Gay Pride marches is on the increase, as is the media coverage of these events.

Lesbians and gays are 'hot stuff' in the media, and the issue of lesbian and gay parenthood is part of the public debate. In September 1995 French television screened a programme on outing, and there has also been a 'Gay Night' on one of the channels. A Swiss documentary on partnership contracts has also been broadcast. At the end of 1995, a programme on lesbian culture focused on the case of a divorced woman who lost the guardianship of her two children to her husband on the grounds of her lesbianism, and followed her battle to get them back.

Homosexuality is becoming less of a taboo, and there is increasing acceptance of lesbian and gay relationships, as seen in the recently introduced registration certificate for lesbian and gay couples. However, social pressure and taboos surrounding motherhood are still very strong. For example, a Belgian lesbian was invited to a congress in Lyon to talk on lesbian parenthood as no French representative could be found.

Legislation

On 14 September 1995, the French Atlantic port city of Saint-Nazaire began issuing registration certificates to lesbian and gay couples. According to Deputy-Mayor Maxime Batard, the document will help gays obtain benefits (currently only available to unmarried hetero - sexual couples) such as access to national health care for a non-working partner, family travel fares and rent subsidies. 'All we have sought to do is give homosexuals the same rights as other citizens,' Batard explained. 'If it can get things moving on a national level, that would be pretty good.' This registration system is being adopted by more and more towns and districts, including three Socialist-led districts in Paris. The national authorities will now have to decide whether to go ahead and open up such programes as the socialized medicine system.

A child with no recognized father is known as a 'natural child', and is not regarded as illegitimate. A single woman with children is not obliged have to have a family council to advise her in case of problems, for example inheritance.

Insemination, adoption and fostering

Insemination is difficult, and a lesbian couple would have to look for an understanding and sympathetic gynaecologist. Some lesbians go abroad for insemination: a counsellor at Jette in Brussels has seen thirty French lesbian couples since she started working there. The information on Jette is circulated in gay circles in France through informal information channels.

Adoption and fostering is limited to married couples, and is not possible for out lesbians. The Gay Parents' Association (APG) recommends that non-biological mothers apply for simple adoption of their partner's child. The conditions for this are that the applicant should be over thirty years of age; there should be at least a fifteen year age gap between the applicant and the child; the biological parent or parents should give their consent for the adoption; and the child should also give her or his consent if she or he is over fifteen years of age. This adoption is more limited than full adoption, as it does not entail any rupture with the family of origin, rather it adds to it. The adopted child remains with the family of origin and does not lose any rights, for example the right of inheritance. The adoption has no effect on the nationality of the child. It can be revoked for serious reason by the judge. This means that a child could have a biological mother and an adopted mother at the same time. Although it is up to the judge to decide that the establishment of a formal link with the applicant is in the best interests of the child, the APG urged non-biological mothers (and fathers) to take advantage of it, arguing that the more lesbian and gay applicants there are, the faster judges will get used to and accept the idea.

Child and family benefits, childcare

This is the same as for single mothers. In 1996, mothers received nothing for the first child, 680 FF for the second and 1,500 FF for three children.

The future

In the coming years, a non-discrimination act may be voted into law which will allow a civil union for *de facto* couples, including lesbians and gays.

Support group

Association des Parents Gais (APG)
BP 253, 75866
Paris Cedex 18
Tel: 33 1 42 40 30 17

Germany

MONIKA WIENBECK

Compiled March 1995; updated February 1996

Statistical overview

Source: *Statistical Yearbook 1992*

Capital: Berlin (since 3 October 1990)
Bonn is the seat of government
Population: 80,974.700: 41,674, 600 female, 39,300, 100 male
63,117,500 (77.95%) in West Germany,
14,391,500 (17.77%) in East Germany and
3,465,700 (4.28%) in Berlin.
Languages: German is spoken by the majority, although there are some Danish speakers (30,000) in Schleswig-Holstein. The largest foreign group resident in Germany (over 8% of the population) speak Turkish, and there are smaller groups speaking Serb-Croat, Italian and Greek. The Serbs (60,000) on the border with Poland speak Serbian.
Religions: Protestant 36%, Roman Catholic 35%, Muslim 2%, non-religious or members of small religious communities (fewer than 1% of the population) 27%
Marriages: 5.8 per 100 inhabitants: East 0.56, West 0.62, Berlin 0.52
Divorces: 29.57 per 100 marriages in West Germany and West Berlin, 7.78 in East Germany and East Berlin
Births: 1.04 per 100 inhabitants: East 0.56, West 1.11, Berlin 8.6 (figures do not include the stillborn)
Deaths: 1.13 per 100 inhabitants.
Infant mortality: 0.61 per 100 live births within the first year, 0.25 within the first seven weeks of life
Life expectancy: 79.8 for women, 73.5 for men (1994)

Single mothers/households headed by women: 2,192,000; 1,310,000 have children younger than 18

General climate and indicators

Lesbian mothers are effectively invisible in both mainstream society and in the lesbian subculture. Thus they often have to cope alone with being a lesbian, a mother and with the issues that arise to do with educating children as a lesbian in straight society. At the beginning of the 1980s, the first lesbian mother's groups were organized in east and west Berlin in an attempt to break through this isolation.

In the 1990s, lesbian motherhood became an issue in mainstream and lesbian media. At least two television talkshows have discussed the issue of gay and lesbian parents, and there have been several reports and interviews with lesbian mothers (and co-mothers) in magazines, a few interviews on the radio and a couple of short reports on foreign events. The western German lesbian magazines published essays on lesbian mothers much earlier, in the 1980s. But the articles came out quite sporadically, and the authors were usually interested in political theory rather than personal experiences. In the past few years, however, the eastern and western media have begun to change their reporting and more frequently publish portraits, interviews and essays about everyday experiences.

Mainstream media has a more general interest in the issue of lesbian motherhood because of two current and related topics: the practice of reproduction technologies and the crisis of the traditional family.

The conservative family model – father, mother (married), children, car, own home – remains the ideal for the majority. But reality is different. The number of divorces is increasing, especially in the West. Nearly one-third of all newborn children are so-called illegitimate children. Many parents are single parents in temporary relationships.

Some of the responsibilities and influences that have traditionally been held by parents have been delegated to other institutions, such as the public education system, television, advisers, and the computer industry.

Moreover, there exists a visible alternative culture: single mothers who do not want to marry, people who prefer to share a flat with friends or live in communities, and so on.

The ideology of traditional family is promoted by Germany's conservative Federal Government. Unfortunately, the propaganda does not match their economic and social policy, which very much favours the independent, ambitious, successful individual on a high salary who is ready to move anywhere at short notice for a good job. Government policy also fails to recognize the reality of people's lives. There are politicians in most parties who recognize the needs of people living in unmarried stable relationships, such as single parents or some gays or lesbians. But these needs figure low on the politicians' list of priorities, and consequently, almost no legislative action is taken. A good example is the work of Berlin's Committee of Justice on the future consitution for the Land. According to the gay protocolist Albrecht Eckert (Green Party), recommendations concerning the rights of homosexuals, single parents and unmarried couples in the new constitution are very likely to be hindered by delaying tactics. Such strategies work quite well, because public pressure is rather weak; most people try to find private solutions to their economic and social problems.

The situation of mothers was and still is different in the former German Democratic Republic (GDR) and West Germany, including West Berlin. The government of the GDR wanted mothers to go back to work soon after the child's birth. Childcare, as well as other support, was easily accessible and used widely. During the day, mothers were encouraged and enabled to participate in public life. Thus, the problem for lesbian single mothers was how to meet other lesbian mothers. And where was she supposed to leave her young child if she wanted to take part in the lesbian groups' meetings, which were usually held in the evenings?

In contrast the childcare provided by the West German and West Berlin communes was generally inadequate. There was no public interest in mothers going to work. Most mothers were married, and if they looked for a full-time job for reasons other than economic, they would be considered selfish and a feminist. For this reason, and because employers assume that women with children take more time off because of their children and are less flexible, they are often first in line when it comes to redundancies. There is also a psychological dimension that distinguishes the people in west from their eastern counterparts, and which involves two more or less internalized ideas.

First, that a biological father, biological mother and their child form a natural unit and therefore belong together. Any deviation is harmful to the child. Second, mother (not father) and child have a symbiotic relationship. The mother has to subordinate her own interests to those of the child and to withdraw from public life. Any deviation is harmful to the child.

In contrast, the Constitution of the Brandenburg Land (former GDR), passed in August 1992, grants single mothers legal protection, stating that: 'Marriage and family are to be protected and supported by the community. Mothers, single parents, and families with many children as well as families with disabled members are granted particular care.' Moreover, the new Berlin constitution of 1995 stipulates that nobody should be discriminated against on grounds of his or her sexual identity, and that long-term relationships that are neither marriage nor family have a claim to protection against discrimination.

When conservative politicians talk about mothers, they are referring to ideological values rather than real people: 'mother' stands as a symbol for a home, keeping the household, reproductive care and altruism; it stands in opposition to anything that has to do with a self-determined or an experimental lifestyle. 'Mother' is also regarded as something weak that has to be protected. Politicians of a different hue, however, acknowledge that looking after your children is a part-time job, and only one of several facets of life. Going to work is another aspect, and is just as important.

In more liberal parts of the Federal Republic the co-existence of lesbians and straight people could best be described as 'live and let live'. Some tolerant straight people respect lesbians' private lives as long as they don't want to change them or society. Nevertheless, there are reasons enough for most lesbians to hide their sexual identity at least in parts of their lives. They may fear that colleagues or workmates, bosses or landlords will discriminate against them. And the children of lesbian mothers often experience discrimination from teachers, schoolmates or schoolmate's parents. In 1994, the case of Cornelia Scheel (the daughter of a former Federal President), evoked a broad public discussion. Cornelia, employed in a senior position by German Cancer Aid, was dismissed because of her relationship with the popular show presenter Hella von Sinnen.

Despite the constant threat of such discrimination, there is little consciousness of, or support for the need of lesbian networks. In Berlin all that exists at institutional level is a small department on homosexual ways of life, where lesbians work on behalf of the other lesbians, one of whom is committed to the cause of lesbian mothers. In the former GDR there were two informal lesbian networks: Berlin's gay and lesbian Sonntagsklub, and the more oppositional, linked lesbian groups which met in the Church's rooms. The Sonntagsklub still exists and is linked with ILGA. The other network is also still operating, but remains effectively invisible, as the members did not establish a formal organization. Many of the network members are mothers, but their political objectives would rather concern single mothers in general than lesbian mothers in particular. The intention was to find a place within heterosexual society rather than within the lesbian community.

In the West Lands and West Berlin, lesbian subculture is dominated by the requirement of political correctness. The first lesbian mother's group, established in west Berlin in 1979, was founded because lesbian mothers felt ostracized by the non-mothers in Berlin's lesbian clubs and at major lesbian events. It was a protest against the stigmatization they experienced simply because of the existence of their children (who were usually regarded as a document of prior collaboration with the patriarchy). Nevertheless, the same subculture was the basis for the development of projects, commercial enterprises, specific media, political organisations or even institutional departments that today, at least in some regions, provide lesbians with the opportunity to work, study or relax in an openly lesbian context. Mothers of sons find it more difficult to participate, since men, including boys from the age of six or eight, are usually excluded.

Legislation

Lesbian partnerships do not appear in the Federal Republic of Germany's laws. Their relationship will not be registered. Since the Federal Constitutional Court refused to continue with this question regarding it as irrelevant to the constitution, most activists have given up hope for any change in the near future. Nevertheless, in Brandenburg, cohabitation is under constitutional protection, and in Brandenburg's and Thuringia's constitutions, discrimination against homosexuals is against the law. These passages are only applicable to matters that are not regulated by federal laws. Rent law, industrial law and civil service law are passed by the Federation.

The rights of political asylum and the rights of aliens are also regulated by federal laws. In this context, because a lesbian is not allowed to marry, she is unable to secure a right of residence for her lover if she is not German by *jus sanguinis*. The rights of aliens are a somewhat extreme example of the wider dilemma that concerns many lesbian activists: namely, that married people's legal rights are sometimes civil rights that should be accessible to anybody. Moreover, a closer look at some privileges reveals that the objective is rather to protect the status of marriage than the individuals in question. For example, the tax bonus *Ehegattensplitting* increases the power of the partner with the higher income and, thus, actually cuts in two ways. (The openly lesbian politician Jutta Oesterle-Schwerin, for example, maintains that marriage always intensifies the power structure in a relationship. Moreover, she argues, German history has shown that assimilation may not help minorities to evade discrimination.) So what is to be called into question: the legal situation of the unmarried or the exclusion of lesbians and gays from marriage?

Lesbian cohabitations with joint children also do not appear in the Federal Republic's laws. A lesbian who has set up a family with her own children and her lover is legally a single mother, and any agreements about shared custody are not recognized. (The two women may complete several contracts, for example regarding the co-mother's right to replace the mother if the latter needs to stay in hospital.) Instead, there are legal relationships between biological father, biological mother, the child and the youth welfare department. Here, the parents are responsible for the child's economic welfare, as the biological origin sets up natural and indissoluble bonds between child and parents. Within this system, lesbian single mothers are a 'deviation' and pose a number of problems.

First of all, a lesbian single mother is obliged to reveal the identity of the biological father, who will then have to pay maintenance. If he refuses, she is supposed to sue for the money in the child's name. If she refuses to disclose the father's identity, at least in West Germany and West Berlin, she will face repressive measures, perhaps even illegal actions. (Following an anonymous tip-off, the social security office of Berlin-Wedding refused public welfare benefits to a woman who refused to name the father of her child). Finally, the state substitutes for the father by paying compensation for the missing maintenance during the first twelve years, and by nominating a public guardian for the child.

In divorce and custody proceedings, an increasing number of judges ignore any information about the mother's lesbianism. But at the same time, the idea of shared custody has become quite popular with the judges and among the youth welfare department's employees. Shared custody does not concern the actual childcare, but rather it grants the authority to sign and to make decisions such as which school a child is going to attend. If a lesbian mother is doomed to this variant and the child stays with her, her former husband will by law have innumerable ways to intervene in her future life. For this reason, feminists are strongly opposed to shared custody, as are some lawyers specialized in family law, but unfortunately, with the forthcoming reform of family law, it is planned to make shared custody the rule. According to the Ministry of Justice, the new laws on custody were passed by the cabinet in March 1996. The next stage is the Bundesrat (conference of Federal German state leaders) and then the Bundestag (Parliament).

As is the case for any working mother, lesbian mothers are protected by industrial law. During maternal or parental leave they may not be dismissed, and their employer must continue to pay their wages (from eight weeks before to eight weeks after the day of delivery). In East Germany, however, the practice of dismissals during leave is apparently widespread, but only a few women are prepared to sue their employer for this illegal action.

Insemination, adoption and fostering

AI may be practised legally by an approved doctor only. In cases where the woman inseminates herself she will not be prosecuted. To practice insemination by an anonymous donor would be very risky for a doctor. The child may take legal steps for compensation because of the (supposed) claim to an inheritance. And if the doctor originally promised the donor anonymity, only to reveal his name at a later date, the donor himself can claim compensation. The Federal Constitutional Court deduced from the constitutional protection of the personality (S 2(1) in conjunction with S 1 of the German constitution) that a child has a right to information about its biological father's identity. The basic assumption is that biological origin is a constituent factor in an individual's personality. There is no constitutional claim to be found which would legitimate a woman's wish to have a child without a father.

Insemination with a known donor may be practised only with married couples and therefore is not accessible for lesbians (unless they are married to a man). A lesbian who wishes to become pregnant therefore has three possibilities: she can evade justice by secretly having an insemination in the Netherlands or in the USA; she may look out for a (usually gay) friend who is willing to be the donor for SI; or she can have sex with a man.

There are no laws against adoption by lesbians. But the selection of the adoptive child's new parents is made by welfare organizations. Relationships without a certificate of marriage are regarded by these organizations as temporary. On the other hand, a reliable relationship is seen as a prerequisite for the happiness of the child. Considering the high number of applicants for a single adoption, lesbians realistically have little chance of success.

Fostering is an option, especially in the case of children who are hard to place, such as HIV-positive children, teenagers or children of drug addicts. However its implementation varies quite arbitrarily from region to region. For example, in the case of one gay couple who moved together with their foster child from a central district to the nearby district of Reinickendorf, Reinickendorf's youth welfare department promptly withdrew the guardianship of the couple.

Among lesbian activists hardly anybody would promote insemination by anonymous donor. Some share the opinion of the Federal Constitutional Court that the child should meet her or his biological father. However, the predominating idea about insemination by doctors is that any reproductive technology is an instrument of patriarchal power. To have a genetic wish list when you buy sperm effectively resumes the fascist ideology of race, and therefore is reprehensible.

Child and family benefits, childcare

Single parents without income have access to either public welfare plus an extra payment for the child, or two years of *Erziehungsgeld* (a child benefit set below subsistence level), plus the difference between this amount and public welfare and the additional payment. *Erziehungsgeld* is granted by the Federation; public welfare and the sum making up the difference is granted by the Commune.

Single parents with their own income have access to the following benefits:

- An allowance on income taxes that varies with the number of children. (Income taxes are raised by the state. Thus, all allowances on taxes are benefits granted by the Federation.)
- A reduced income tax *(Steuerklasse II)*.
- A child allowance granted by the Federation *(Kindergeld)*.
- *Erziehungsgeld* during parental leave (maximum duration two years).

Since 1 Janunary 1996, the *Kindergeld* does not vary according to income. People with a high income may choose a tax reduction *(Kinderfreibetrag)* instead. Both the child allowance and the tax reduction are accessible only for people with their own income or for married couples with at least one income. And both mean money from the state.

People with no income do not receive any child allowance from the state. They do not profit from the new laws, since the laws concerning what the communes pay have not changed. The federal law leaves them discretionary powers.

With tax reductions calculated in percentages, people with a high income receive more money for their children than those on a low income. With the *Ehegattensplitting*, married couples assess their taxes together, benefitting in proportion to the income differences between the two of them, so marriages with high income differences are rewarded. *Ehegattensplitting* is also called *Patriarchenlohn* – wages for the patriarch – because men with high incomes married to women with little or no income make the most profit out of this regulation.

The laws on tax reduction do not really support marriage or family. They rather increase the social and economic differences in our society between the poor and the rich, and between men and women. Needless to say, co-mothers have no access to any benefits.

If the biological father does not pay maintenance, the mother may receive money in advance. The sum differs with the age of the child, and it is higher in West Germany and West Berlin than in the former GDR. The sum increased by 20 per cent on 1 January 1996.

Public childcare in the Federal Republic is the responsibility of the Communes. In West Germany the facilities' capacity is too low to satisfy the demand. In some Communes a mother has to apply for a place in nursery school immediately after the child is born. If she moves somewhere else the vacant place will be lost. In many Communes there is no public care available for children younger than three years of age. Moreover, the extent of care often means that women can't accept full- time jobs: in places other than the very big cities, nursery schools are usually open for just half a day.

In East Germany, vacancies in public childcare are no longer guaranteed, but the situation is much better and people tend to send their children to day nursery quite early. Again, the statistics reveal differences between the two parts of the Republic. In the east, more than half (56 per cent) of all children up to the age of three are sent to a public day nursery. In West Germany the figure is 3 per cent, and the 50 per cent mark is exceeded in West Germany when children are aged four to five.

According to a decision of the Federal Constitutional Court, a mother can claim a place for her child in nursery school. However, towards the end of 1994, the Communes began a series of public campaigns declaring that they would not meet the January 1996 deadline set by the Federal Government. As a result, in early 1996, an information brochure released by the Federal Ministry for Family, 'Senior Citizens, Women and Youth' stated: 'Despite enormous efforts this claim cannot be put into effect according to the schedule in every Land'. Parliament and the Bundesrat subsequently agreed upon an interim solution, conceding that public childcare should be accessible only at one or several qualifying dates per year; and that the communes may also fulfil the claim with 'offers of the same value'.

The future

For a long time, the lesbian subculture of both western and eastern Germany has failed to acknowledge the figure of the lesbian mother. And role models for lesbian mothers, as well as attractive ideas about her power and her identity, are yet to be found. The first moves have been made by lesbian mothers' groups and by the organizers of public events on the issue.

Indeed, some activists are also trying to correct the legal situation by establishing precedents. Hopefully supported by representatives of the more liberal European Union member states, they have considerable prospects of success in making gay and lesbian partnerships generally and officially recognized, perhaps within the next ten or twenty years.

Support groups

SLP e.V.
(Bundesarbeitsgemeinschaft schwuler und lesbischer Paare –
National Workgroup of Gay and Lesbian Couples)
Hauptstr. 48
30916 Isernhagen FB
Tel: 49-4106-78552

Lesbenring
(national lesbian organization, dominated by women from western Germany and West Berlin)
Bonner Talweg 55
53113 Bonn
Tel: 49-228-24 13 57

UFV
(Unabhaengiger Frauenverband – 'Independent Women's Association', dominated by women from eastern Germany)
Anklamer Str. 38
10115 Berlin
Tel: 49-30-44 3412 03
Fax: 49-30-558 55 42

Greece

IRENE PETROPOULOU

Compiled December 1995; updated March 1996

Statistical overview

Source: *CIRCA*

Capital: Athens
Population: 10,500,000 (1994)
Language: Greek
Ethnic groups: Greek (9,600,000), Macedonian (150,000), Turkish (90,000), Albanian (60,000) and others.
Religions: Christian Orthodox 98%, Muslim 1.5%, other (Roman Catholic, Protestant, Jewish) 0.5%.
Divorces: 8,650 (1986)
Births: 10 per 1000 (1993)
Deaths: 10 per 1000 (1993)
Infant mortality: 8 per 1000 (1992)
Life expectancy: 80.6 for women, 75.6 for men (1994)

General climate and indicators

In Greece, public attitudes towards lesbians, and homosexuality in general, remain negative. Society's attitude is: Do what you want in private but don't make a public issue out of it. As a result, lesbians tend to adopt a low profile.

Lesbianism has become a favourite subject for the media but not all the coverage promotes a positive image, and there has been no discussion of the issue of lesbian mothers. Society regards the lesbian as unfit for motherhood, believing that her sexual lifestyle will influence the sexuality of the child. Unsurprisingly, then, lesbian mothers prefer to avoid seeking public attention for fear that they may be taken to court and lose custody of their children.

Lesbian mothers are also virtually invisible on the lesbian scene, and there is only one lesbian mother active in EOK (the Greek Homosexual Community). Most find that they are regarded with suspicion by other lesbians, often because they were married for a period of their lives and lesbians think of them as possibly deciding to be straight at some time in the future. On the other hand, many lesbians would like to have children. The usual solution for lesbians is to get married, mostly to a gay man who would also like children. There are no provisions, at the moment, for insemination.

EOK is a movement which aims to promote a positive image of gay men and lesbians. Its work includes running a help line offering help and advice to other lesbians and gay men, monitoring the press for coverage of lesbian and gay issues and protesting accordingly. The Women's Caucus of EOK is responsible for manning the help line for half of the week, preparing lesbian issues to be broadcast in EOK's hourly radio programme, once a week, and generally answering other lesbians' questions.

Legislation

There is no legislation that is directly aimed at lesbian mothers. In Greece, lesbian relationships have no legal status. The general attitude in the courtroom is that lesbians are unfit mothers, which in custody cases involving lesbian mothers gives the husband a lot of negotiating power. He can choose whether or not to bring up the mother's lesbianism as a reason for granting him custody of the children.

Insemination, adoption and fostering

There is no access to donor insemination, adoption or fostering for lesbians. These are rights granted to heterosexual couples only.

Child and family benefits, childcare

There are child and family benefits, but these are meant only for heterosexual mothers. A lesbian mother should not reveal her sexual orientation if she wants to have access to these benefits. In other words, she should pretend to be an unmarried mother.

The future

There is currently no lobbying activity on the part of EOK for changes in legislation or for new legislation, for example on recognition of same-sex partnerships. EOK intends to work on this in the near future.

Support group

The only group that can help a lesbian mother facing problems is EOK.

Irene Petropoulou
Coordinator of the Women's Caucus of EOK
PO Box 26077
100 22 Athens
e-mail: sappho@acrogate.ath.forthnet.gr

Hungary
JENNIFER C. BROWN
Compiled March 1996

Statistical overview

Source: Office of Statistics

Capital: Budapest (pop. 2,016,000)
Population: 10,200,000
Languages: Hungarian (official), Romani, German, Slovak
Ethnic groups: Hungarians (90%), Gypsies, Germans, Slovaks, Croatians, Romanians
Religions: Roman Catholic 67.5%, Protestant 25%, Jewish, atheist and others 7.5%
Marriages: 5.4 per 1000
Divorces: 2.4 per 1000
Births: 11.7 per 1000
Deaths: 13.8 per 1000
Infant mortality: 13.2 per 1000
Life expectancy: 73.74 for women, 65.67 for men
Single mothers/households headed by women: 15%

General climate and indicators

In 1992 when Free Democrat MP Dorottya Bky introduced a clause on sexual harassment, she was laughed at by her own party. Today, women and lesbians still have little support in the government and a grassroots movement is only just starting to gain a foothold. Indeed, when it comes to women's issues, Hungary is still about twenty-five years behind the West. No one looks twice at one advertisement for a local beer, where a husband, facing a glass of beer for dinner asks,

'Where is a woman who can cook like this?' In a climate where the traditional family model is heavily idealized, acceptance of lesbian and single motherhood is low despite the high divorce rate. Two organizations, NaNE and the Feminist Network have provided a place for many lesbians to come out, but many feminists would like to distance themselves from lesbians and many lesbians don't have a political, feminist identity.

Hence, lesbian motherhood is not dealt with separately as a social issue from single motherhood and virtually no precedent exists for AI or adoption for lesbians. Lobbying efforts on behalf of gays and lesbians is virtually non-existent and opportunities for lesbians to network with each other are few. While many new clubs exist for gay men, few have successfully organized an evening especially for lesbians.

Yet some initiatives have recently emerged. Hungarian lesbians meet at Cafe Capella every other Thursday night and a club called Bad Boys has just begun to have a women's night on Saturdays. A consciousness-raising group has been set up at the O'vegylet AIDS foundation on Friday nights and the Feminist Network is planning a women's centre with a library. Although more symbolic than active, the Szivarvany Foundation is the most well-known organization for gays and lesbians. A hotline called Meleg Ha'tta'r (Warm Background) was founded in 1995 to help with crisis counselling for gays and lesbians and is considered to be the only active organization especially for lesbians and gays, functioning as a source for information about gay life and HIV testing.

Legislation

Up until 1987, homosexuality was punishable with up to five years in prison. Today, Section 199 of the Penal Code includes a higher age of consent for lesbians and gay men (eighteen) than for heterosexuals (fourteen) with prison terms for violations of up to three years.

In March 1995, the Constitutional Court directed the Parliament to pass a new law that gave virtually all benefits, currently only enjoyed by heterosexual domestic partners, to gay and lesbian couples. While the domestic partnership law will still not enable couples to adopt, it is not clear whether the law will include matters of child custody or AI. To date, Parliament has not yet complied with the Constitutional Court's decision, but it is expected to hold a debate and pass the law sometime in 1996.

Child and family benefits, childcare

One area currently under review is benefits for single mothers. Parliament has debated a bill on pregnancy and child support that would affect maternity leave and state support payments for infants. Under the proposed legislation, some childcare payments will be phased out after 15 April 1996. While pregnancy aid would be universally available, other forms of support will depend on income status. The bill calls for a 2,000 forint ($14.30) rise in monthly infant care support to 9,600 forint ($68.50). Infant care support will only be paid to those families with a per capita monthly net income below 19,500 forint ($139.20). Instead of a maternity supplement, a single sum of 10,000 fiorint ($71.40) will be introduced as financial support. Maternity leave will last up to twenty-four weeks, and be equal to 60 to 70 per cent of average earnings. The plan to discontinue the pregnancy supplement and replace it with a lower maternity leave sum has received much objection from opposition party members. It goes without saying that a loss in benefits will cause the greatest difficulties to single mothers.

Support groups

Meleg Ha'tta'r
1854 Bp. PF 50
Tel: 302-5080

Hungarian Feminist Network
Forach u. 118
1139 Budapest

Women for Women Together Against Violence (NaNE): provides legal counselling, shelter and support for battered or sexually abused women.

Szivarvany (Rainbow) Association, the first legal group for gays and lesbians in Hungary:
Tel: 111-0651

O'vegylet: Zichy Jen utca 29
Tel: 111-0651

Publications

Masok: A monthly magazine geared strictly toward homosexual men, though recently, classified ads and services geared toward lesbians are beginning to appear.

Nszely (Female Person): Formed by the Women's Section of the League of Independent Trade Unions, Green Women's Group, Society of Women Entrepreneurs and Feminist Network in September 1991. Contains information about current political, legal and social issues affecting women in Hungary. Address: 1399 Budapest, Pf. 701/1092

Ireland

PATRICIA PRENDIVILLE

Compiled June 1995

Statistical overview

Source: National Statistics Office

Capital: Dublin

Population: 3,525,719: 1,772,301 women; 1,753,418 men (1991)

Languages: English, Irish

Ethnic groups: Indigenous traveller community; 3,878; Jewish community 1,581

Religions: Roman Catholic 98%, Protestant 1%, other 1%

Marriages: 4.4 per 1000 population

Divorces: Divorce not available

Single: 1,953,445

Married: 1,329,428 (includes first marriage, widow(er)s and people married following dissolution of previous marriage)

Deserted: 23,685

Marriage annulled: 1,221

Legally separated: 11,152

Other separated: 12,982

Divorced in another country: 6,103

Total separated: 55,143

Births: 13.9 per 1000, to unmarried women; 19.5% of all births (1993)

Deaths: 8.9 per 1000 population

Infant mortality: 5.9 per 1000 births, 4.0 per 1000 neo-natal births

Life expectancy: 76.7 for Women 71.01 forMen (1987)

Women: 1,772,301

married: 667,051
> **single:** 921,693
> **separated:** 33,793
> **widowed:** 149,764

Actual number of mothers not available.
Single mothers/lone mothers: 39,403 (1994)
Households headed by women: 270,427 (1991)

This profile on motherhood and particularly lesbian motherhood in Ireland is correct at the time of writing (June 1995). Various legislative changes, educational initiatives and social changes are indicated which will alter the situation here. It should also be noted that while there are various facts and numbers, laws and state instruments in place to support motherhood, lone motherhood and the rights of children, the entire subject is viewed differently in various groups, classes, locations and age groups. Secondly, the social perspective on the various issues raised in the profile varies enormously. This is written by a feminist, mid-thirties, rural middle-class, employed, child-free lesbian.

General climate and indicators

The Republic of Ireland has a constitution which covers various aspects of what are usually referred to as 'women's issues' – in other words, the family, women working outside the home if they have children, divorce, succession rights, rights of children.

There have been enormous changes in the past twenty to thirty years around these various issues, both constitutional and legal. Thus, while there is still a constitutional ban on divorce, there is a very clear judicial separation process, with excellent conditions, ease of attainability and protection for children, women and men.

The family is given a special status in the constitution as the cornerstone of society, which should be protected by the laws of the state. This has formed the backdrop for the debate about divorce, the status of children and rights for women. There is no divorce legislation in Ireland – it is constitutionally banned, as of 1995. There is a proposed referendum scheduled for November 1995. Second families are therefore irregular in that the heterosexual couple is not married. This population is put at approximately seventy thousand by the Divorce

Action Group. Since 1987, the succession rights of children from all relationships have been protected so that second families have equal rights to those of the children of the marriage.

Family Law reform has focused on the rights of women, the rights of children and succession rights. Many of these changes have emerged as the result of demands, lobbying and campaigning by women's groups.

Motherhood is traditionally considered a vocation, set in the context of marriage it is desired by all women and protected by society. One particular constitutional protection sought to remove the need for mothers to work outside the home for financial benefit, since the work of rearing children is seen as so crucial to the state. This led to a marriage bar operating within the public service sector until the mid-1970s, the existence of mother and baby homes from where the babies were adopted, and created financial difficulties and the social stigma of lone motherhood. This has all changed now. There is no marriage bar (which was never really about child-rearing, but to keep married women out of the workforce). Adoption rates have drastically decreased, even though there is still a very high proportion of babies born outside of marriage. Mother and baby homes have all but disappeared, and there is a lone parents allowance which is paid to all lone parents, regardless of how their situation arose. Overall, the social stigma is very much reduced.

Lesbians remain a fairly invisible group in Ireland on the whole. While the Gay and Lesbian Equality Network (GLEN) ran a very public campaign and lobby to repeal the legislation on male homosexuality, the non-inclusion of lesbians in that legislation meant that lesbianism was not an issue in the public debates and discussions. As with practically all other countries and cultures, female sexuality is not readily perceived as independent of men, therefore two women are not part of the thinking.

Since 1991, the organization of lesbians in Ireland has become much more coherent and structured. A group called Lesbians Organizing Together (LOT), formed in the same year, campaigns on various issues of relevance to lesbians in an attempt to raise the profile of lesbians in Ireland more generally, as well as providing a social service to the lesbian community. The increase in the representation of lesbians in magazines, British-based soap operas and popular culture have all contributed to a greater awareness within families of the existence of Irish lesbians. Nevertheless, the issues particularly affecting lesbians and lesbian mothers in Ireland remain, influencing their lives emotionally and financially.

Legislation

Parenthood is governed by various family law and status of children acts.

Married heterosexual parents are both deemed to be parents of the child, whose birth is registered by the hospital authorities, and both names appear on the birth certificate. Joint guardianship is automatic. With unmarried heterosexual parents, the father, if he wants these rights, initially has to establish his fatherhood of the child, and he can then apply separately to the Registrar of Births, Marriages and Deaths to have his name included on the certificate.This does not, however, confer any rights on the father, rather, these accrue to the child, who has the right of succession to the father's estate. The father has to apply to the courts for guardianship rights, access and custody. The mother is the automatic guardian. An unmarried woman is considered the sole guardian, and her name is automatically included on the birth certificate. The status of illegitimacy was abolished in 1987 by the Status of Children Act. The mother cannot record the father's name without his consent.

Other significant changes in the law include the Decriminalisation of Male Homosexuality Act 1993; the incitement to Hatred Act 1989 (which includes homosexuality as a category where it is illegal to incite hatred); and the Unfair Dismissals Act 1994 (which amended Employment Law to include sexual orientation as a category covered by the law). There is, however, no legal status for lesbian or gay relationships and no registry of partnerships, whether heterosexual or homosexual. Lesbian groups, separated heterosexuals in second relationships and civil rights activists are campaigning on these issues.

Custody of the children of lesbian mothers is at the discretion of the courts. Under the various laws, the judge assesses custody on the basis of the best interests of the child/children only, and does not take into account sexual orientation. However, hearsay evidence is admissible, and women are rightly fearful of declaring their involvement with another woman in court, as they might lose custody. Nevertheless there have been a number of reported cases where the lesbian mother was open about her sexual orientation, and the children were still awarded to her.

AI custody cases have not arisen, at least not publicly, in Ireland, as yet. To date, AI has had a low profile, and is seen as a reproductive technology that is used to help infertile heterosexual couples.

Insemination, adoption and fostering

Access to donor insemination is predominantly by private routes, and only one clinic publicly provides AI for women, heterosexual couples and lesbian couples. Most lesbian couples make private arrangements with male friends, or friends of friends. Some have legal arrangements to cover the questions of maintenance, access, the donor's relationship with the child, now or in the future, and clarification of the legal position. Other lesbians have sex with a man or men in order to become pregnant without first discussing it with them.

Adoption for lesbian couples who are open about their relationship is not available in Ireland. Single women are also excluded from adopting. The position is the same for fostering, although single women may in exceptional circumstances act as foster mothers – 'professional fostering' rather than 'family fostering'. However, on the whole, fostering and adoption is meant for heterosexual couples, with clear guidelines laid down about the mother working outside the home, which couples must satisfy to be eligible. The adoption organizations are private voluntary bodies in the main, with denominational groups operating within the field. Fostering is arranged by Regional Health Boards – state agencies.

Child and family benefits, childcare

A children's allowance is paid to every mother on a per head basis whether married or unmarried. This money is not taxed, and is to be used by her as she sees fit. Family benefits accrue to families who are below a designated poverty line. Benefits include heat and coal allowances in the winter, clothing allowances, discretionary payments for exceptional bills or expenses, a medical card which entitles the family to free medical care and prescriptions, and rent allowances.

Lone Parent Allowance is paid by the Department of Social Welfare to all lone parents, whether unmarried, separated, widowed or a prisoner's spouse. There used to be distinctions made between the various categories, but this has been changed.

A second layer of benefits accrues to families whose earned income means that they have lost the additional benefits listed above. The benefits include a topping up of the wages to a specified minimum, a hospital card to qualify for certain medical expenses benefits, and a reduced rent allowance. This is known as Family Income Supplement.

Childcare facilities in Ireland are predominantly private and expensive, and not allowable under tax or expenses. Often it is a relation who does the childminding, usually the grandmothers. Otherwise people either employ a child minder to come into the home or leave their children at creches or the child minder's own home. Pre-playschools can be found in the larger towns and cities, and these are also used extensively. Most parents make arrangements that suit their circumstances. There is a system of health board pre-schools. but there is usually a very long waiting list and priority is given to children who are at some risk in the home.

The bigger companies, semi-state organizations and interested private/voluntary organizations sometimes provide workplace creches, but these are seen as a perk rather than a right.

Campaigns are currently being waged on these issues, especially the issue of tax relief for the expense of buying childcare.

The future

The Second Commission on the Status of Women, 1993, recommended: that lesbian organizations be funded (successful in 1995); that lesbians be recognized as a discriminated group among women; and that no discrimination on the basis of sexual orientation be allowed.

The Council for the Status of Women (CSW) at their 1995 AGM adopted six lesbian motions ranging from funding, to positive action of representation, to eliminating homophobia. It remains to be seen how these translate into action. Motions based on the Lesbian Equality Network (LEN) campaigns for the inclusion of lesbian motherhood rights, equal rights for partners regardless of sexual orientation, succession and next-of-kin rights for lesbian partners were also adopted by the CSW.

The forthcoming Equal Status Act should include sexual orientation, but the lobby on this is still operating. The Departments of Equality and Law Reform have been visited and lobbied, but no acceptance of proposed changes to the Bill presented has emerged to date. It is hoped that the CSW will continue to lobby on this with LEN and LOT (Lesbians Organising Together), who have both lobbied separately, and who are affiliated to the CSW.

Research on lesbian and gay poverty was published by the Combat Poverty Agency (CPA) in 1995. This research was undertaken by GLEN, with funding from the CPA, and involved questionnaires and interviews with two hundred lesbians and gays. The results confirmed the thesis that lesbians and gays experience discrimination which disproportionately affects their quality of life, job prospects, mental and physical health and sense of well-being. There is also statistical evidence to show that lesbians and gays are disproportionately financially impoverished according to educational achievements. The research will have important consequences in terms of acceptance into those Community Development programmes which other discriminated groups in Ireland participate in and network around.

The Second Commission on the Status of Women has recomended a proposal to include lesbian and gay sexual orientation in these modules that form part of the school curriculum dealing with sex and relationship education. The Commission also proposed that the Law Reform Commission look into the proposals around next-of-kin nomination for all non-married couples, and the establishment of a Department of Women's Affairs to monitor the implementaton of their recommendations.

Support groups

Lesbian Lines in Cork, Dublin, Limerick, Galway, Belfast, Derry, Waterford.

Lesbian and Gay groups in Dublin, Cork, Limerick, Waterford, Belfast, Derry, Sligo, Drogheda, Kilkenny, Wexford, Dundalk.
Council for the Status of Women, National Umbrella Group for Women's Organisations, based in Dublin.
Lesbians Organising Together (LOT),
5 Capel Street
Dublin 1
tel: (353) 872 7770

Dublin-based umbrella organization, with offices providing meeting space, discussion groups and outreach.

Lesbian Mothers Groups, contact LOT also known as New Beginnings

Lesbian Equality Network (LEN): contact LOT offices.

Parents Support: contact Gay Switchboard, Dublin, tel: (353) 872 1055.

Most of the colleges and universities have lesbian and gay societies.

Publications

Equality Now for Lesbians and Gay Men, Irish Council for Civil
    Liberties, Dublin 1990
Dublin Lesbian Line, Submission to the Second Commission on the
    Status of Women, Dublin 1991
LOT annual reports, LOT, Dublin, 1993, 1994
GLEN and Combat Poverty: Lesbian and Gay Poverty Research,
    CPA, Dublin 1995 (forthcoming)
LEN submission to the Department of Equality and Law Reform,
    Dublin 1994
Second Commission on the Status of Women, Final Report, Dublin,
    Stationery Office, 1993
Out for Ourselves, Women's Community Press and Dublin Lesbian
    and Gay Collectives, Dublin 1986
Gay Community News, monthly free newspaper
Ms Chief no. 9 1995, interviews with lesbian mothers

Italy

DANIELA DANNA

Compiled August 1995

Statistical overview

Sources: *Rapporto Annuale: La Situazione del Paese 1993*, by Istituto Nazionale di Statistica, Roma *Stato dell'Italia*, (ed. by Paul Ginsborg), Il Saggiatore, Milano 1994

Capital: Rome

Population: 57,153,695

Languages: Italian, small German minority in South Tirol, other very small minorities speaking French, Greek, Albanian. Widespread use of dialects or, more correctly, regional languages (14% of the population speaks only in dialect).

Ethnic groups: Italians; foreigners who officially reside in the country are 6 per thousand, and mostly come from the Maghreb countries. A much higher number is estimated for immigrants without papers: 3–4% of the population (1–1.5 million).

Religions: 85% Roman Catholic, most of the others are atheists, 1% Evangelical Protestants. 30% of the population attends Mass every week, 97.9% is baptized, about 83% of marriages are in the religious form.

Marriages: absolute number: 292,173

Divorces: absolute number: 14,944, plus 31,181 *separazioni* (less definitive form of marriage interruption which becomes a full divorce after some years)

Registered same-sex partnerships: No law or public registers exist at the time of writing, but forthcoming in Pisa. Informal registers at local clubs of Arci Gay Arci Lesbica and at the office for the Counsellor of the Mayor of Rome for homosexual issues (no numbers given).

Births: 9.4 per 1000 (with 1.2–1.3 more girls than boys. Italy has the lowest number of children in the world calculated on the whole female population).

Deaths: 9.5 per 1000

Infant mortality: 7.4 per 1000

Life expectancy: 80.2 for women, 73.5 for men

Single mothers/households headed by women: up to sixty-five years old: 2,123,000 (881,000 living with children); total: 2,691,000

General climate and indicators

The political advance of the right wing forces (*Alleanza Nazionale*, the former new facist party, and *Forza Italia*, made to magically appear by the tycoon Berlusconi a few months before the 1994 elections) came to a stop with the April 1995 elections. The new majoritarian system was decreed winner. The *'Progressisti'* is a liberal coalition composed of the former Left, the Communists and the Greens, together with sections of the Christian Democracy and Liberal centrist parties.

The rhetoric of the rescue of the traditional family, that brought the introduction of a new Ministry of the Family, has been brought to a halt. The ministry has been renamed the Ministry for Social Solidarity and is headed by a woman. But Catholicism is the adhesive force in the propaganda of the coalition. The *Progressisti* intend to provide govenment funding for private, that is Catholic, schools. Legislation permitting abortion is under review and homosexual unions are not admitted into the concept of the 'family'.

Because of the lack of a social security system, the family is still an important resource in times of economic difficulties. The rate of unemployment is currently 12 per cent, and much higher among the youth and women. The young people's rebellion against the family in the 1960s and 1970s is now almost non-existent. 'Mother' is still the primary identification offered to women, and even feminists, the majority of whom follow the *pensiero della differenza,* insist on the importance of maternity both as a symbol and in reality. Women who choose to be single mothers are rare and only one per cent of heterosexual couples living together are not married.

Lesbians have received more and more positive coverage in the media, which has helped to establish a recognized identity and more respect in social life. However, many lesbians still choose to conceal their sexuality, fearing attacks from the family or the loss of their jobs, though there are court cases establishing that sexual orientation cannot be used as a reason for dismissal.

Lesbian mothers are attacked by the press when they use alternative methods of insemination. In 1988, when Benedetta and Donatella from Milano gave an interview to the gay magazine Babilonia about the child they had conceived in a clinic, a major daily paper wrote about the case and the rest of the press followed, mostly with outraged comments. But the women stood up for their choice, providing a very dignified and autonomous portrait of lesbians.

In 1994, following an interview with gynaecologist Ambrassa, who revealed that he had helped a lesbian couple to conceive a child, the issue of lesbians bearing children became front-page news. The accent was put on the need for a regulation to prohibit insemination of single women and lesbians. The gynaecologist was subsequently suspended from membership of Cecos, an organization of gynaecologists dealing with new reproductive technologies. The National Committee for Bioethics (a formal body with consultative status, established in 1990 by the Prime Minister) expressed a majority in favour of the prohibition of insemination outside the heterosexual couple, claiming defence of the child's right to a father. A project of law signed by the PDS, and with the woman president of the environmentalist association Lega per l'Ambiente as first proposer, is proposing this principle. Only a Communist Party proposal, also signed by members of PDS, recognizes single women's right to access to reproduction technologies. The women of Arci Gay Arci Lesbica, the national lesbian and gay association, responded by spreading information about SI.

Legislation

The question of lesbian mothers and the law concerns primarily their presence in the law as homosexuals. Italy does not possess an extensive list of laws prohibiting homosexuality, as its repression was considered an area reserved for the Catholic Church. All the laws protecting public morals can be used against homosexual behaviour displayed in public, as was the case in Agrigento in 1981 when two women were sentenced to six months in prison merely for kissing in a public place. Lesbians in public employment also fear a norm obliging them to maintain 'decent' behaviour. (It is a norm rather than a law, because it has been put forward by a minister.) However, there have been no recent cases of the use of this norm, either against homosexuals or other people. The only public explicit reference to homosexuality appears in a norm from the Ministry of Health, put forward when AIDS started to become an issue in Italy, and which is still in force. This prohibits all 'homosexuals' and lesbians from donating blood. The new norms have led to a significant drop in blood donations.

Italy has no anti-discrimination law dealing explicitly with lesbians or gays, but jurisprudence around work issues has recognized the anti-discriminatory principle even in the case of homosexuals.

Divorce legislation does not mention sexual orientation. The best interest of the child is the leading principle in deciding who gains custody, while the concept of paternal authority in the family was changed in 1975 to an egalitarian division between husband and wife. Lesbian mothers and gay fathers tend to hide their sexual orientation in court because the courts' attitude is generally not liberal. Lawyers continue to advise lesbian mothers to keep silent, even if hiding means that they become subject to blackmailing by the ex-partner. There have been instances of psychological harassment of lesbians in child custody cases, but the issue has not come out in the press, not even the gay and lesbian press. On the other hand, a gay man was awarded custody of his fifteen-year-old son in 1995 in Latina, when the son testified his desire to continue living with his father.

Lesbian relationships currently have no legal recognition, although this is changing. Since the mid-1980s, there has been a tendency to recognize a man and a woman living together without being married as a couple in a sort of minor marriage. In 1993, a court in Torino gave a gay couple the same consideration as a cohabiting heterosexual couple by allowing one of the men the right not to testify against the other. This decision has since been cancelled by the Superior Court.

In early 1996, the Council of Pisa province approved a motion recommending that the Italian Parliament should make a law for lesbian and gay civil unions; and that, in the meantime, the municipal councils of the Pisa province should register lesbian and gay couples. The municipality of Pisa is expected to be the first in Italy to have a register.

Insemination, adoption and fostering

SI is still virtually unpractised, but there is some interest: a translation of Lisa Saffron's handbook on SI, with the title *Autoinseminazione*, was published as the first title of a new women's publishing company in 1995; and there are instances of lesbian couples using clinics for insemination by a gynaecologist. However, the overwhelming majority of lesbians with children have conceived them in heterosexual unions.

There is no law regulating insemination, which is practised in public hospitals only with the semen of the husband, (based on a 1985 directive by the Ministry of Health), and without norms or guidelines in many private clinics. Catholics are against all forms of alternative insemination, including its practice in public hospitals.

Until April 1995 the clinics were free to treat whoever they wanted. Following the public debate about new reproductive technologies, however, the National Council of the Federation of Physicians approved a regulation forbidding all physicians to inseminate anyone other than heterosexual couples. The severest penalty for failure to comply is expulsion from the Federation, which effectively prohibits a doctor from practising in Italy. This has been greeted with enthusiasm by the Minister of Health, but with protest by the Left, which insists that an internal corporation regulation should not take the place of a state law.

Adoption was reserved for married heterosexuals until the recent case of the famous actress Dalila Di Lazzaro, who wanted to adopt a child as a single person. In March 1994, the Constitutional Court, applying the 1967 International Convention of Strasbourg's decision to allow unmarried persons to adopt a child, granted Di Lazzaro permission to adopt. A corresponding national law has not been approved yet.

Anyone who has a room in which the child or children can live, and who is judged suitable by social workers, can qualify for fostering. A lesbian child psychiatrist living with her partner in Genova has fostered a couple of children and has spoken about the experience on television and in the press. Nobody ever questioned her right or ability to foster together with her partner.

Child and family benefits, childcare

Although there is much discussion about the need to increase the birth rate (now under substitution level), there is no policy giving economic advantages to families. The only benefits are tax deductions for each child, which are double in the case of single parents. Some local authorities, for example in South Tyrol, give families an amount of money for each child born, but this is not very widespread.

Public childcare is clearly insufficient in most of Italy and private care is extremely expensive.

The future

The desire to become a mother is increasing within the lesbian community, as is the desire for fatherhood in the gay community. Assuming that the political situation does not degenerate, it is likely that a network of potential mothers and fathers practising SI will develop.

The Resolution of the European Parliament in February 1994 started a widespread debate around lesbian and gay issues in Italy, including parenting. A campaign was started in March 1995 by two gay associations, Arci Gay Arci Lesbica and Azione Omosessuale, gathering signatures in favour of their proposed law introducing *unioni civili*. This was a very important moment for the visibility of the lesbian and gay movement in Italy, marking the start of a dialogue with Italian citizens that showed people the faces and bodies of real homosexuals and lesbians instead of some media stereotype. Generally people wanted to sign, having been reassured that the law did not include adoptions.

This attitude towards adoption led to conflict within the gay movement. Some gays talked to the press about their desire to become fathers by adoption, while the movement's leaders emphasized that nobody was seeking the right to adopt. For lesbians however, the possibility of adoption was crucial, as it would allow their children to have two legal parents, and pressure was exerted on the lesbian and gay associations to include the issue of two-mother families in their proposal for a law recognizing gay and lesbian couples. The proposal, presented in Parliament by all the parties of the left and some members of *Forza Italia*, included only the institution of registers of *unioni civili* for both homosexuals and heterosexuals, which accorded the partners the same position as a husband and wife for most legal and succession matters. There is an alternative proposal, signed only by the Communist Party, that will give homosexual couples the possibility of adopting children.

Unfortunately the likelihood of getting laws of this kind approved in the short term is really low, as the Catholics refuse absolutely to officially recognize gay and lesbian couples. The Pope's message is that people of this orientation must remain chaste. Only a few priests object publicly to this decree and support the gay Catholic groups that have been formed in different cities.

By 1 July, 1995, Arci Gay Arci Lesbica had gathered 70,000 signatures, which they presented during the second national demonstration of gays and lesbians in Bologna. Together with the first march, which took place on 2 July 1994, when over ten thousand homosexuals and supporters marched through the streets of Rome, this represented the biggest gay and lesbian demonstrations Italy had ever seen. There was an equally successful gathering in Naples in 1996.

The publicity around the resolution provoked a backlash, and a new anti-gay movement, the Defence Committee for the Family Following Natural and Christian order, was formed. It had gathered about 70,000 signatures against the European Parliament Resolution by September 1995, and its petition aimed 'to stop publicity and legalization of so-called homosexual families; and to protect our families with correct laws that respect natural and Christian principles on which our European civilization is founded'. It continued:

> With your help, and with God's help, we will continue this campaign, until the day on which our pressure on the political authorities has full success, deleting at last and for ever this abominable Resolution, and replacing it with a new and true law, meeting the interests of the real and right Italian and European family.

Support groups

No official group for lesbian mothers has been set up as yet. Women at CDM, via Cicco Simonetta 15, Milano, have tried to start one, but events aimed at lesbian mothers, such as a party for Mother's Day, have been poorly attended.

Latvia

NICOLA WILLIAMS
Compiled September 1995

Statistical overview

Source: Office of Statistics, Year 1994

Capital: Riga
Population: 2,600,000
Language: Latvian
Ethnic groups: Latvian 54.2%, Russian 33.1%, others include Belorussian, Ukranian, Polish, Lithuanian
Religions: Lutheran, Roman Catholic, Rusian Orthodox,
Marriage: 4.5 per 1000 (total: 11,572)
Divorce: 7.3 per 1000
Births: 42,192
Deaths: 41,624
Infant mortality: 16 per 1000
Life expectancy: 74.8 for women, 63.2 for men

General climate and indicators

Following Latvia's renewal of independence in 1991, lesbians and gays have established organizations and infrastructures such as bars, clubs and shops. Cultural, educational and social events are held and various lifestyles freely developed. Latvian society has not acquired a high level of tolerance, however – no doubt a consequence of fifty years of totalitarianism. Since 1992, there have been a number of violent attacks against individuals in lesbian and gay bars and cafes in Riga, many of which have been closed down as a result. Police representatives frequently conduct unauthorized raids on lesbian and gay

establishments under the pretence of checking documents or searching for weapons, while both lesbians and gays are often attacked in the
streets or at meeting places.

No official statistics exist regarding the number of lesbians in
Latvia. The Riga-based Latvian Association for Sexual Equality
(LASV), formed in November 1990, boasts forty members, just 10 per
cent of whom are women. According to LASV board member Juris
Lavrikovs, while homosexual orientation among men in Latvia was
recognized by society in 1994, lesbianism is still thought by many not
even to exist. 'My mother is sixty and for her to learn that men could
be gay and what that meant was shocking enough. It would be impossible for her to even comprehend that women could be attracted to
other women,' he points out.

The few lesbians who are acknowledged as such are stereotyped as
either 'crazy, ill or prostitutes'. 'People say to me "Poor you! You are
ill!",' says Astrida Indricane, a 21-year-old lesbian currently living in
Riga. Baptized a Roman Catholic, she applied to study at the Catholic
Seminary in Riga in 1994. Her application was turned down because
she was a lesbian: 'I was told I had to choose between my studies or
my sexual orientation. For me, there was no choice.'

Legislation

On 5 February 1992, the Supreme Court of the Republic of Latvia
adopted legislation to repeal Paragraph 124.1 of the Criminal Code
banning male homosexuality. No reference at all is made to lesbianism
in any legislative material. LASV believes the change in law was
not, as portrayed, an attempt to end discrimination based on sexual
orientation, but rather a reflection of Latvia's will to join the Council
of Europe, which it could not have done with such legislation in place.

In September 1993, however, Paragraph 35.2 of the Family Law in
Civil Court Law was adopted, banning both marriages among same-
gender individuals and all same-sex relationships – including, by
inference, lesbian relationships, and marriages. This law is directly
contrary to the European Parliament's resolution 'On equal rights for
homosexuals and lesbians in the European Community', which Latvia
undertook to uphold to after signing an associate agreement with the
EU on 12 June, 1995.

Repealing Paragraph 35.2 is not an end in itself, however. In Latvia, housing registration procedures prohibit two lesbians or gays from living lawfully in one apartment. For that reason alone, Astrida Indricane is unable to live in Latvia with her girlfriend Brigit Brohingen, a thirty-year-old horticulturalist currently living in Germany. In the first same-sex (illegal) wedding to be conducted in Latvia, Astrida and Brigit married on 12 August 1995 in the Old Town of Riga. The service was conducted by a Swedish Lutheran woman priest, already excommunicated from the Lutheran Church in Latvia for her public acceptance of homosexuality. After the street service, the wedding party laid flowers by Riga's Monument of Liberty, erected in 1935 as a tribute to Latvia's new-found freedom and unity. The couple are now living together in Germany.

To date, no court case yet exists to set a precedent regarding the custody rights of lesbians with children from a previous heterosexual relationship. By law, both mother and father are entitled to custody of the child, although in practical terms, economic status decides most cases.

Insemination, adoption and fostering

In Latvia, lesbians have no right to raise children. They have no access to donor insemination, adoption or fostering. The privately run Latvian Family Centre in Riga hopes to introduce an in vitro fertilization (IVF) programme into its clinic in September 1995 – the first such insemination programme to be made available in Latvia. IVF treatment will only be available to married couples, however. By law, it is only married couples who are likewise able to adopt and foster children.

The future

> For us, our rights as mothers and the number of lesbian mother support networks are not even issues as such yet. They are rights that we will fight for much, much later on our agenda. At the moment, we are simply fighting to be recognized, respected and treated as equal citizens in Lativa. (Astrida Indricane)

In January 1995 the LASV embarked on an anti-discrimination project funded by the EU's Phare and Tacis Democracy Programme. LASV's main goals are to found a lesbian and gay information centre and to lobby Parliament to adopt lesbian and gay equality in all legislation.

In 1994 the Latvian parliamentary Human Rights Commission failed to respond to LASV's proposals for amendments to the Latvian Criminal Code. Consequently, in June 1995 LASV submitted new proposals to the President of Latvia, the Parliament and to the Commission. Their proposals call for an immediate change to existing law to ban discrimination based on sexual orientation; and for legislation to be accepted to allow the registration of same sex partnerships in Latvia.

In December 1995, Riga, hosted the ILGA's seventeenth European Regional conference.

Support groups

No lesbian mother support networks, lesbian custody projects or play groups yet exist in Latvia. For advice, practical help and support, contact:
Latvian Association for Sexual Equality (LASV)
Puskina iela 1a
Riga LV 1018
Tel: 371 2 223 293
Publishers of Latvia's only gay and lesbian magazine, *Loks*, can also be contacted at the above address

For information regarding donor insemination and other medical matters, contact:
Latvia's Health Support Centre for Lesbians and Gays,
SEMMES
Puskina iela 1a
Riga, LV 1018
Tel: 371 2 223 950

Lithuania

MAUREEN SHARP
Compiled September 1995

Statistical overview

Source: State Office of Statistics

Capital: Vilnius
Population: 3,717,700, 69% urban (1995)
Languages: Principle: Lithuanian. Others: Russian, Polish
Ethnic groups: Lithuanian 80%, Russian 9%, Polish 7%, Belorussian 1.5%, Ukrainian 1%
Religions: Roman Catholic 85%, others include Russian Orthodox, Lutheran, Jewish
Marriages: 6.3 per 1000 (1994) (Decreasing, from 9.2 in 1991, 8.0 in 1992, 6.4 in 1993)
Divorces: 3.0 per 1000, or 47.4 per 100 marriages (1994)
Births: 12.5 per 1000 average population, decreasing (15.2 in 1990, 15.0 in 1991, 14.3 in 1992)
Deaths: 12.5 per 1000, 14.4 for males, 10.8 for females
Infant mortality: 13.9 deaths under one year per 1000 live births
Life expectancy: 74.93 for women, 62.79 for men (1994)
Mothers: Estimate 1114 women per 1000 men. 50.8 per cent of families had one child under eighteen in 1994, 39.7 had two, 7.3 had three, 1.5 had four, 0.7 had five or more
Single mothers: 120,000 (out of 600,000)

General climate and indicators

As head of the Assistance to Family branch of the Ministry of Social Security and Labour, Aldona Kariciauskiene recognizes that a democratic Lithuania should be tolerant of alternative family models. It is a wistful sentiment which is occasionally heard among activists in this Baltic country, but one which is not reflected in legislation or in general attitudes. 'This is a Catholic country, so we have a traditional family,' explains Kariciauskiene. She has no objection to women wanting to cohabit, but finds the idea of registered lesbian marriages difficult: 'I can't imagine what the purpose of this would be. They can't have their own biological children, and traditional families are for bringing up children.'

Lesbianism is only now beginning to be discussed in the press. Because homosexuality was not spoken about for so long, public opinion is shaped by misinformation and stereotyping. In April 1995 the AIDS Centre conducted a survey into the attitudes towards homosexuality of 500 Vilnius teenagers. This revealed that only 19 per cent of the participating sixteen and seventeen year-olds believed that gays and lesbians were normal, and 43 per cent believed that homosexual intercourse should be a criminal act.

Nijole Steponkute, an advocate for women and mothers, explains that to be lesbian in Lithuania is 'a shame, and a mental sickness. You are seen as dirty and immoral.' Understandably then, lesbians are very closeted – so much so that many people do not believe they exist. Gledre Purvaneckiene, who is the adviser to the government on women's issues, could not find five lesbian women to fill seats reserved for them at a Nordic forum. Ironically, Steponkute is aware that at any one time, at least three women out of the Lithuanian delegation were, in fact, lesbian. One lesbian mother told me 'I feel such controversy inside me. I would like to just forget that I'm lesbian and be like a normal person. But I can't.'

Very broadly speaking, single mothers are accepted as normal and are not the subject of much discrimination. However, tradition dictates that there is much more sympathy for divorced women than for single mothers who have never married. The ideology of motherhood in Lithuania contains conflicting attitudes which place great pressure on women. First, it is assumed that women can only fulfil their true role within a traditional family structure: 91 per cent of men and 94 per cent of women agree that what most women really want is home and children. Women bear the lion's share of the child-rearing, and 84 per cent of men and 91 per cent of women also believe that a pre-school child is likely to suffer if his or her mother works. Yet 68 per cent of men and 73 per cent of women also believe that women should contribute to the household income. In effect, society is telling women that they must be mothers and they must work, but that working makes them bad mothers.

Legislation

The first Baltic country to gain independence, Lithuania was the last to repeal Article 1 of the Soviet Penal Code, under which homosexuality was a criminal act punishable by up to three years in prison. Its repeal was accomplished on 3 July 1993, largely under pressure from the Council of Europe, which Lithuania was at the time vying to join. The Soviet Family and Marriage Code is still in effect in Lithuania, though small changes have been made, and other sections are not enforced. A new code is expected by 1996.

The prevailing belief that a child needs the influence of both a mother and a father shapes present legislation, and will continue to do so in the new code. In all custody cases, the courts are primarily concerned with what is best for the child, and after one year of age the parents have equal rights and responsibilities. Once the child reaches ten years of age the court will consider her or his placement preference.

Though both biological parents legally have equal rights (regardless of whether or not they are married), tradition dictates that mothers generally receive custody. The Ministry of Justice does not keep data on the number or outcome of custody cases, but the Department of Statistics lists 110,000 children as living only with their mother, and 10,000 as living only with their father (this includes widows and widowers as well as divorced and unmarried men and women). No woman seeking custody of her children has ever been revealed to the courts as a lesbian.

Insemination, adoption and fostering

According to the head of the Family Planning clinic in Vilnius, Dr Vytautas Klimas, the Catholic Church and the group 'Doctors Pro-Life' exercise a great deal of prohibitive control at the Ministry of

Health with respect to AI. Though the procedure is not illegal, doctors are prevented from offering the service by their economic dependence on the Ministry of Health. Dr Klimas is instead focusing on changing legislation, and hopes to have the procedure legalized by the end of the year. Until this happens, he will cheerfully refer families to Dr Valentinas Matulevicius in Kaunas, the only doctor in Lithuania who openly provides donor insemination. Dr Matulevicius applauds the efforts of Dr Klimas, but expresses doubts about the viability of the campaign for accessible and legalized insemination: 'The situation is worsening; religion is exerting a greater and greater influence at the Ministry of Health.' The total cost to families for five cycles of treatment is approximately 200 USD.

In the absence of legislation governing access to AI, Dr Matulevicius is guided by his own criteria. In eight years of practice, no woman has ever cited lesbianism as the reason for requesting AI. If she did, Dr Matulevicius admits that he would probably refuse her. He doesn't treat single women either.

The latest statistics now available show that 1,855 children lost parental support in 1993 (only 17 per cent of whom were orphaned). Only 115 of these were adopted. For this reason, Dr Genovaite Babachinaite, Head of the Department of Criminology at the Lithuanian Law Institute, believes that it is not difficult for single women to adopt children. However, no data is available on the success rates of single women's applications for adoption.

There is no legal barrier for lesbian women wishing to adopt, but it is doubtful that such a situation would be looked upon favourably by the governmental organizations which screen applicants. Certainly, a lesbian couple could not jointly adopt a child, because a child cannot legally have two mothers. There has been no publicized test case. The situation for fostering is exactly the same as for adoption.

Child and family benefits, childcare

On paper, there are a total of 109 social benefits for families with children. Rima Shatkute, a psychologist who works at the Lithuanian Women's Centre, believes that most of the population are aware of about eight or nine of them. Lilja Vasiliauskiene, Director of the Vilnius Women's Home, explains that the application processes are so complicated, the clerks so hostile, the queues so long and the mental and physical exertion of collecting stamps and papers so exhausting that even women who are aware of what they are entitled to often opt to forego their benefits. Enforcement problems also abound. For example, women can take up to three years off work with benefits after bearing a child, and her job is legally guaranteed for this time. In practice, this is true only in the public sector, and not always even there.

During Soviet rule, over 60 per cent of children below school age attended childcare institutions known as kindergartens. By 1993, this number had dropped to 20.5 per cent. There were 1,681 such establishments in 1990; only 927 in 1993. The greatest loss has been in rural areas, where 577 of 854 kindergartens closed between 1990 and 1993. Aldona Kariciauskiene explains that although parents are required to pay only 60 per cent of the cost of meals in pre-school institutions, even this fee (approximately 10 USD per month) is too much for many families, especially if they have more than one pre-school child. Further, she confesses that closures have meant that it is often difficult for mothers to find a place, even if they can afford it.

The future

Progressive legislation cannot be expected in this century. There is not even a proper debate at this time. The most hopeful sign is perhaps that people are beginning to become aware of the presence of lesbians in Lithuania. Whether this revelation will cause a backlash or initiate constructive dialogues is yet to be seen.

Support groups

There are currently no lesbian mother support networks, lesbian custody projects, discussion groups or playgroups in Lithuania. There is one lesbian activist group in the process of forming called Sapho, but the founder refused to be interviewed for this piece. According to one lesbian, the group does not welcome lesbian mothers, because the founder does not believe mothers can be 'real lesbians'. The founder is closeted, so does not wish her name to be used, but she can be reached in the Lithuanian city of Ignalina at (370 29) 440 166. She does not speak English.

There are currently six lesbians registered with the Lithuanian Gay League (LGL). LGL has office space and a library in Lithuania's only permanent gay bar, Amsterdamo Klubas, which is situated at 18 Basanaviciaus gatve in Vilnius, tel (370 2) 651 638. The chairperson is Vladimir Simonko, who works alongside Eduardas Platovas, the co-ordinator of the Lithuanian branch of the joint ILGA and Phare project. Both are extremely active and receptive, and are eager for the input and participation of lesbians.

The Lithuanian Movement for Sexual Equality (LMSE) is working on legislation, especially in the Criminal Code, but has no lesbian members. The group is run out of the AIDS Centre in Vilnius and is mainly concerned with AIDS prevention and education. There is some conflict with LGL, which is much more active. LMSE is chaired by Aleksandras Zolotuchinas, who can be reached through the AIDS Centre at (370 2) 350 465.

Giedre Purvaneckiene, in addition to her job as adviser to the government on women's issues, was the Chairperson of the Commission for the Fourth World Women's Conference held in Beijing in September 1995. She is extremely receptive to enquiries, but has no contact with the lesbian community. Her office number is (370 2) 622 053.

The Women's Society of Lithuania is an extremely well-connected advice centre for women seeking anything from legal advice to free psychological consultations. It is especially involved in helping women with children. If nothing else, this is the best place to go to find out just what is available. The chairperson is Nijole Steponkute.

Women's Society of Lithuania
20-11 Besanaviciaus gatve
Vilnius
Tel: 370 2 650 386

The Netherlands

SHELLEY ANDERSON
Compiled October 1994; updated March 1996

Statistical overview

Source: *Statistical Yearbook, 1992*

Capital: Den Haag/Amsterdam

Population: 15,129,150 (women: 7,648,728; men: 7,480,422)

Languages: Dutch, Frisian

Ethnic groups: Dutch, Turkish, Surinamese, Indonesian

Religions: Protestant, Catholic, Muslim (3%), Hindu or Buddhist (0.6%)

Marriages: total: 93,638 per 1000: 6.2

average age at marriage: women 28.8, men 31.5

Divorces: total: 30,463 per 1000 married men: 8.6

total divorce rate: 29.3

(average number of marriages that would end in divorce if the same death and divorce risks observed in the calendar year applied in the future)

Registered same-sex partnerships: 35,000 samesex couples (1989) 8.5 % of non-married couple households

Births: Total live births: 196,734 per 1000: 13 per 1000 women (in the 15 to 44 year age group): 56.6

average age of mother: 29.6

number of boys born per 1000 girls: 1052

Deaths: per 1000: 7.3 (women: 6.6; men: 8.1)

Infant mortality: total: 1,235 per 1000 live births: 6.3

Life expectancy: 80.3 for women: 74.3 for men

General climate and indicators

No one knows how many lesbian mothers there are in the Netherlands. An estimated 35,000 same-sex couples were living together in 1989, which was about 8.5 per cent of the total number of non-married couples households (with or without children). Anouk Mulder cites a figure of 60,000 women, who identify as lesbians and are bringing up children (*Wordt er een Potje van gemaakt? – Is a Mess Being Made?* An investigation into the legal position of lesbian couples with children in Dutch law, 1992, quoting from research published by Professo. Robert A.P. Tielman in 1982).

While there are no specific laws that prohibit lesbians from becoming mothers in the Netherlands, a Dutch lesbian mother's lot is not necessarily a happy one. Lesbians cannot marry one another; cannot adopt children (nor can any single individual, homosexual or heterosexual); the partner of a lesbian mother cannot be granted custody of any child or children the lesbian couple may be co-parenting.

Several government studies have, however, proved rather positive for lesbian mothers. In 1986 the Nederlandse Gezinsraad (Dutch Family Council, a government advisory board) released a report by Dr T. Kras on 'Children of Homosexual Parents'. Kras stated in her report that, while there may be some experiences of stigmatization and conflict in some children, the sex role and psychological development of the children of homosexual parents does not differ from that of children raised by heterosexuals; and that children raised by homosexuals do not become homosexual themselves any more often than children raised by heterosexual parents. She concluded her report by dismissing the idea that a homosexual parent was a bad parent *per se*; it was the personal qualities of the individual rather than any sexual preference that made a parent adequate or not.

Another advisory report,'Parenthood without Discrimination', this time from the Raad voor het Jeugdbeleid (Council for Youth Policy), appeared in 1988. This also concluded that homosexuality was no bar to good parenting; the only specific problem about growing up in any non-traditional family was the possibility of being stigmatized by society.

In 1991, the Emancipatie Raad (a government council that deals with questions of women's advancement in society) issued a report suggesting that lesbian co-parents should have the same legal opportunities to be recognized and become guardians as unmarried men have. The Emancipatie Raad introduced the concept of `social parenthood' – parents who are unrelated by blood but who care for children – and argued that the rights of such co-parents should be protected by law.

Legislation

Article 1 of the Dutch Constitution states that discrimination on the grounds of religion, belief, political ideas, sex, race `or on any grounds whatsoever, shall not be permitted'. The courts have interpreted this to mean that discrimination based on sexual preference is illegal.

On 1 September, 1994, the Algemene Wet Gelijke Behandeling (Equal Treatment Law) came into effect. This law states that people must be treated equally in work and business situations, regardless of their sex, nationality, race, sexual preference, religion, marital status or disability. The government appointed a commission (Commisie Gelijke Behandeling) to make determinations about complaints regarding violations of the new law. Individuals (including private citizens and judges) or institutions can request an opinion from the commission in operation from 1 January 1995. These opinions can be submitted during a court case. While judges do not have to follow its opinion, a favourable determination by the commission will usually strengthen a case. Since sexual preference is covered, there is a feeling that the new law might be used to improve the legal situation of lesbian mothers. No cases regarding lesbian mothers have yet been taken to court under this law.

In the Netherlands, the biological mother is the legal guardian of her child. If the mother is married, her husband is the legal father of the children, whether he is the biological father or not. This legal relationship *(familierechtelijke betrekkingen)* between parent and child has – often automatic – consequences in terms of inheritance, nationality, responsibilities regarding support and maintenance, the right to a certain last name, guardianship and custody. A lesbian co-parent *(meemoeder)* can sometimes be granted certain supervisory rights in regard to a child (for example, the right to safeguard financial matters until the child is old enough to handle her or his own financial affairs), if the biological mother requests this.

One Dutch lesbian couple, after having their request for joint parental authority over their children rejected by the Dutch Supreme Court (on the grounds that the non-biological mother was not legally a parent), took their case to the European Commission of Human Rights. In May 1992, the Commission rejected their case, stating that, 'as regards parental authority over a child, a homosexual couple cannot be equated to a man and a woman living together'. (Kerkhoven, Hinke and Hinke vs. The Netherlands, 15666/89).

Lesbian co-parents have been denied equal rights to guardianship by Dutch courts, despite the fact that, since 1985, a man in an unmarried heterosexual relationship can recognize any children from the relationship as his, and receive equal guardianship, as long as the mother does not object.

In two different opinion polls conducted in the early 1990s, approximately half of the Dutch population supported the idea of allowing lesbians and gay men to marry. Unmarried couples, whether same-sex or heterosexual, can have a legal contract drawn up (a *samenwoning*, or 'living together' contract) which gives them many of same rights enjoyed by married couples. Such contracts can include property rights, social security and pension rights, inheritance and next-of-kin visiting rights in hospitals or jails (in general, the Dutch do not create any problems about homosexual partners visiting their lovers in hospital or prison). While this contract is only legally binding between the couple themselves, 'some employers (including the state itself) do award some (or even all) "spousal" benefits to those who have entered into one'. (*Homosexuality: An EC Issue: Essays on Lesbian and Gay Rights in European Law and Policy*, Kees Waaldijk and Andrew Clapham, eds, 1993). Increasingly in the Netherlands, little legal distinction is made between married couples and unmarried couples who live together (especially in the areas of rent protection, income tax and social security).

To be legal, marriages must be registered at the local city hall. Religious marriages are not recognized in the Netherlands, although the Remonstrance Church (a small Protestant denomination) does bless same-sex relationships. In 1994 two American lesbians travelled to the Netherlands in order to be married in a Remonstrance ceremony in Alkmaar, an event that made the local newspapers. In June 1991, the city hall of Deventer officially registered a lesbian couple (the first Dutch same-sex couple allowed to do so). By 1996, 125 Dutch towns and cities allowed same-sex couples to register their partnerships, but these registrations are not legally binding.

The lesbian and gay communities are divided about whether being allowed to marry is a suitable goal or not. Some argue that marriage is imitating heterosexuality; others support individualization – the belief that social benefits, taxes and pensions should be accorded to individuals regardless of their marital status. Dutch gay liberation organizations have argued against the partnership legislation developed in Scandinavian countries that allows lesbian and gay couples to register in a separate partner register and grants almost the same rights as the marriage register. This is precisely their objection, as they call not for 'almost the same rights' but for 'exactly the same rights'. The COC (the national Dutch lesbian and gay rights organization) has organized day-long public debates on whether the lesbian and gay rights movement should support homosexual marriages.

The Minister of Justice appointed a commission to investigate the ways in which unmarried couples could be extended equal rights. This Advisory Commission for Legislation (Commisie voor Toetsing van Wetgevingsprojecten) published its report (entitled 'Leefvormen', or 'Family Forms') in February 1992. The commission proposed two different forms of registered partnerships to protect the rights of unmarried (same-sex or heterosexual) couples: a `light' registration, that would extend unmarried couples the same social security and tax rights as married couples; and a 'heavy' registration, which would confer all the legal benefits of marriage (including divorce, maintenance and pension rights). The commission, however, recommended that legal parenthood and adoption be available only to heterosexual couples. In April 1995, the Amsterdam City Council sent a letter urging the Dutch government to grant gay couples equal rights in the areas of parenting, adoption, kinship, inheritance and alimony.

Insemination, adoption and fostering

No one knows how many lesbians have become mothers through donor insemination, though it is probably more than anyone realizes.'

During the period 1977-90, a medical centre in Leiden recorded, the births of 740 children by donor insemination; 15 per cent of these births (or 112 babies) were to lesbian mothers. Another hospital in Leiden reported that 10 per cent of the donor insemination cases it had handled since 1984 involved lesbian mothers, and that approximately 120 children were born to lesbian mothers by donor insemination from 1984 to 1990. These figures do not include SI.

The Leiden clinic has developed an approach to AI that holds the middle line between an anonymous and a known donor. With this alternative method, which is neiither official nor promoted but rather suggested personally to certain candidates, the donor remains anonymous but is willing to deposit certain information about himself with a notary. The child, and only the child, can later retrieve this information, as well as the identity of the donor, if she or he wants to.

There is an unwritten law in the Netherlands, (not official policy but always applied in practice), that the age limit for insemination is forty. Many older women go to Belgium to be inseminated.

Mira de Jong, an employee of the (SAD)-Schorer Foundation, a social service organization for lesbians and gays, feels the number of lesbians wanting access to insemination is likely to increase. In the past, many lesbian women discovered their lesbianism only after they were married, and had children from these heterosexual marriages. Because of the more open atmosphere today, women learn about their sexual identity earlier, and do not go into heterosexual marriage. This means that having children becomes a more conscious, deliberate choice.

The ease or difficulty of access to donor insemination depends to a large extent on where you live. 'It's really a problem outside the big cities,' de Jong explained. 'The situation is not altogether perfect.' It is up to the discretion of medical facilities whether or not they will allow lesbians to be inseminated: many such facilities refuse to do so. Lesbians learn what hospitals to go to through word of mouth, or by reading books like *Tips voor two Moeders: Lesbische vrouwen kiezen voor kinderen (Tips for Two Mothers: Lesbian Women Choosing Children)*, edited by Vera Mulder, 1989. This includes the addresses of ten sympathetic Dutch medical facilities, and notes that the list is not complete because 'not all facilities are willing to publicly state that they provide donor insemination to lesbians, for fear of being overwhelmed by "hordes of lesbians wanting children"'. The book recommends raising the question even with unsympathetic hospitals, in order to draw the attention of unwilling authorities to the issue, and to discover the occasional sympathetic doctor who will refer the woman to a more progressive medical facility.

In 1994, a major Dutch medical facility in Amsterdam (the Kunstmatige Inseminatie Donorzaad, or KID,) announced that, due to a shortage of sperm donors, lesbians would be placed at the bottom of a long waiting list of those desiring AI.

Lesbians cannot legally adopt children in the Netherlands. Adoption is covered in the Civil Code (Burgerlijk Wetboek) in Book 1, Article 227. In general, only couples who have been legally married for five years can adopt (the exception being if a couple has applied to adopt a child, and, within three months of the application, one of the partners dies, the adoption may still go through). Since lesbians cannot legally marry, they cannot adopt.

In 1988, there was a long discussion in Parliament about whether or not it was desirable to open up adoption to other than married couples. There was a specific debate on adoption by lesbians and gay men, which was covered in the mainstream media. One argument against was that the exporting countries (India, Brazil and Sri Lanka) would stop sending orphans to the Netherlands if they knew homosexuals could adopt. Research was conducted into the legal situation in other countries. Considering that no country allowed homosexuals to adopt children, the government concluded that 'the interest of the child must come first. ... the government does not think it desirable that homosexuals adopt children, because this could block the balanced development of the child...'. Fear was expressed that children with same-sex parents might grow up to `idealize' the other sex, which could cause problems in the child's development.

Homosexuals can and do foster children in the Netherlands. In 1992 the Centrale voor Pleegzorg (Central Council for Foster Care) stated that it placed about 250 children per year in lesbian or gay households.

Child and family benefits, childcare

Although the divorce rate has risen in the Netherlands, with one out of every three marriages ending in divorce, and with more and more younger people living together without being married, family life remains important. The traditional idea of the family as a married man and wife with several children is very much alive. While every Dutch mother, no matter what her sexual preference or marital status, is eligible for child benefits from the government, there is a serious lack of affordable childcare centres. The Netherlands has the lowest rate of women with children working outside the home in the entire European Union.

The future

Many people interviewed felt confident that the legal situation for lesbian mothers would improve under the new coalition government. For the first time in over a decade, the Conservative Christian Democrats are no longer in power. The new government is composed of parties like the PvDA (Labour Party), the D'66 (centre-left), and the VVD (more conservative party), some of whom have in the past supported lesbian and gay issues in Parliament.

In October 1995, *Euroletter* reported that Justice Parliamentary Undersecretary Mrs Schmitz in a letter to the Dutch parliament presented the government's ideas on laws concerning relationships, adoption and family. The main point of her letter, referred to as the *Nota Leefvormen*, was that she favoured neither the opening up of marriage to gays nor the adoption by single parents of a foreign child, contrary to a ruling in a Dutch court in spring 1995 allowing the adoption of a Brazilian girl by a single Dutch woman. In her view, adoption by single parents and gay couples would lead to negative reactions from other, especially third-world, countries from where most children up for adoption in the Netherlands originate. Instead she proposed to allow adoption in these cases only when the adopted child is Dutch. But as only some forty Dutch children are put up for adoption each year, with demand much higher, and Dutch law stating that the natural mother has to agree with the family adopting the child, it is expected that the natural mother of the child will in the vast majority of cases prefer the child to grow up with a heterosexual married couple.

Despite this, in 1996 the first step was taken in the Dutch parliament to open up civil marriage to lesbian and gay couples, and in March 1996, *Euroletter* reported that all three Dutch coalition parties were in favour of the legalization of lesbian and gay marriage.

Support groups

There are a few good books available. *Tips voor two Moeders: Lesbische vrouwen kiezen voor kinderen (Tips for Two Mothers: Lesbian Women Choosing Children)*, edited by Vera Mulder, 1989 includes detailed practical information on SI and donor insemination, including the legal implications of known and unknown donors. Interspersed between chapters like 'Questions for Donors' ('What are your reasons for donating sperm?', 'Are you willing to take a fertility test? To practise safe sex?', 'What kinds of illnesses run in your family?') are nine interviews with lesbian mothers.

Another popular book is *Wel kinderen, Geen man: Lesbisch en 'alleenstaand' moederschap (Children Yes, Husband No: Lesbian and Single Motherhood)*, by Anke van Dijke and Linda Terpstra, 1991.

Gay and lesbian health-care workers in cities like Leiden, Utrecht and Amsterdam sometimes form working groups that provide information or materials of interest to lesbian mothers. The SAD-Schorer Foundation offers periodic day-long events, with workshops on how to cope with being a lesbian and a mother, too; how to choose the best school for your child; available social networks; legal questions and donor insemination. Originally aimed only at lesbians, the events are now open to both lesbians and gay men.

The lesbian mothers group in Utrecht is very interested in contact with lesbian mothers around the world. Write:

J. Nieboer
Padangstraat 42
NL-3531 TC
Utrecht

The COC (national Dutch lesbian and gay rights organization) lobbies for the rights of lesbian mothers as part of its mandate. Local COC branches may offer social events and information for lesbian mothers. The address of the national office is:

COC
Nieuwezijds Voorburgwal 68-70
1012 SE Amsterdam
Tel: 31 20 623 1192
Fax: 31 20 626 7795

Aletta is a women's health centre that offers periodic information sessions for lesbians who want to learn more about becoming mothers.
Aletta
Maliesingel 46
3581 BM
Utrecht
Tel. 31 30 312850

Norway

GRO LINDSTAD
Compiled April 1995; updated August 1995

Statistical overview

Source: National Statistics Office, for 1993

Capital: Oslo
Population: 4.4 million
Languages: Norwegian
Religions: State church, Lutheran Protestant
Marriages: 20,605
Divorces: 10,934
Registered same-sex partnerships: 136: 87 male, 49 female
Births: 60,092 (born out of wedlock: 44.4%)
Deaths: 44,071
Infant mortality: not known (very low)
Life expectancy: 80.64 for women, 74.88 for men
Single mothers/households headed by women: 153,094
Families: 2,019,388 (includes single households – they are defined as families)

General climate and indicators

Politically the family is still considered a very important part of Norwegian society. As far as the issue of lesbian motherhood is concerned a poll carried out at the end of 1992 showed that 73 per cent of those asked were against lesbians being foster parents, and 75 per cent were against them being given the right to adopt.

Legislation

In 1993, Norway was the second country in the world to introduce a partnership law granting lesbian and gay couples the same legal, social and economic obligations and rights as heterosexual married couples. The only differences are that lesbian and gay couples cannot be 'married' in church, and the law confers no rights regarding children.

Norwegian law gives only heterosexual couples the right to adopt. The right to insemination as part of the public and private health system is also limited to heterosexual couples. There is no law setting clear restrictions as to who can be foster parents, this is decided in each county by the individual boards on social services. These boards consist of elected politicians. Those lesbians who are life partners of lesbians with children have no legal rights to these children, even when there is no known legal father.The only existing court case material concerns matters of child custody after divorce, when the other party has cited the mother's lesbianism as grounds for divorce.

In summary, we can see a clear pattern in Norwegian court decisions. In cases brought before the court where it is clear that the mother is comfortable with her sexual identity and is open about her lesbianism, she is given custody. When the mother has problems dealing with her lesbianism, custody is usually given to the father.

Insemination, adoption and fostering

Lesbians have no legal right to insemination, but there is nothing positively forbidding it either. So, those lesbians who want children just practise SI, mostly with known donors and in many cases with gay men or male friends. To a certain degree donors are also found through advertising in lesbian and gay publications. Some lesbians also travel to Denmark, where the attitude over the years has been more liberal.

There are no known cases of lesbians being allowed to adopt. And there are no current plans to change the adoption law in Norway. This law was revised in 1986 and upheld strict rules as to who could adopt.

There are examples of lesbian foster parents, but the prevailing attitude is negative, due probably to lack of information combined with general prejudice. Whether or not lesbians and gay men should be allowed to be foster parents arose as a matter for political discussion in the city council in Oslo in 1994. Members of the Christian Democratic Party wanted a strict rule for the county of Oslo specifying that only married heterosexual couples were fit to be foster parents. None of the other political parties supported this proposal. Nethertheless, the Christian Democrats, who are members of the Norwegian Parliament, vowed to pursue their proposal to ban lesbians and gay men as foster parents by tabling a law amendment. At the time of writing there have been no more developments in this matter.

On a positive front, the Department on Children and Families said in a letter to the Oslo city council that it would be unwise to make a decision that would ban lesbians and gay men as foster parents.

Child and family benefits, childcare

The political climate has shown concern for single mothers by voting through a set of regulations providing economic support. A single mother is eligible to receive a set amount per month if she chooses to stay at home with the child or children until they reach the age of ten.

Another sum, available to everybody with children, is paid once a month and per child until the child reaches the age of sixteen. Everybody is also entitled to a minimum of child support per month. This is then eventually enforced from the obligors by the Norwegian authorities. The set of regulations concerning single mothers is under revision and will be presented within a year.

Childcare is provided by both public and private daycare centres. Payment is on a sliding scale, where those with low income can apply to pay less. Single parents can apply preferentially for childcare in the daycare centres.

The future

The Norwegian lesbian and gay movement is working to make lesbians and gay men more visible as both parents and caretakers of children. If society allows us to work with and care for other people's children in our capacity as, for example, teachers, social workers, why can't we be regarded as suitable foster parents or adoptive parents?

Most pressing is the situation for those children growing up with two lesbian mothers, where there is no known legal father. Work has to be done to secure both the rights of the children and the non-biological mother. Adoption offers the best solution, but given the political climate in Norway today, this is a legal change that lies in the future. Journalists have contacted the Norwegian National Organization for Lesbian and Gay Liberation (LLHPB) to confirm that working for adoption is the organization's next big issue. This is a question that will be put to the organization's National Convention in May 1996.

Support groups

Lesbiske Mødregruppe
PB 752 Sentrum 0106
Oslo
A group for lesbian mothers.

Homofile og barn
PB 6838 St Olavs pl 0130
Oslo
A mixed group of lesbians and gay men that works politically to make the groups visible as parents and caretakers of children.

LLH PB
6838 St Olavs pl 0130
Oslo
The Norwegian National Organisation for Lesbian and Gay Liberation.

Poland

THOMAS E. LAVELL III

Statistical overview

Source: Central Statistical Office (GUS) *1995 Demographic Year Book*

Capital: Warsaw (Warszawa)

Population: 38.6 million (1995)

Languages: Polish; small communities of German, Lithuanian, Ukranian speakers in border areas with those respective countries, tens of thousands each.

Ethnic groups: German, Lithuanian Ukranian. Between 7000 to 10,000 people declare themselves to be Jewish

Religions: Roman Catholic (95–97%); Orthodox, Lutheran and Jewish

Marriages: 207,689; 5 per 1000 (1994)

Divorces: 31,574 (1994)

Births: 481,285 (1994)

Deaths: 386,398 (1994)

Infant mortality: 1523 per 100,000 live births (1994 total 7284)

Life expectancy: 76 for women, 67 for men

Single mothers/households headed by women: Total in 1988 (most recent figure available): 1,395 million households of a total 10,948 million households

General climate and indicators

Early in 1996, the Constitution of Poland was entirely rewritten to replace the Soviet-imposed constitution, which was heavily amended as a result of the socio-economic changes of the 1989–90. Labour and social policies emphasize a child-rearing, homemaking role for women, neither recognizing men's roles in families nor allowing women to work in certain professions (often better paid) on the grounds of an alleged higher risk to their health. As a result, cases of discrimination abound.

Polish law makes no mention of homosexuality. However, the social climate, heavily influenced by the Roman Catholic upbringing of the vast majority of Poles, encourages lesbian women and gay men to remain in hiding, particularly in the workplace. Press reports on lesbian and gay issues, while sensational in the past, have been more even-handed in the mid-1990s, but issues relating specifically to lesbians have generally been ignored by the press (including the gay press) and by society at large. Lesbian activism, after an initial surge in the early post-communist years, and in cooperation with gay men, has waned.

The rest of this chapter combines material from the Polish Committee of NGOs (Beijing 1995) and from an addendum to that report by the Polish Lesbian and Gay Movement (RLG) based in Warsaw.

Legislation

Article 67 Part 2 of the Constitution grants all citizens of the Republic of Poland equal rights, regardless of sex. Article 78 states that women are granted equal rights to men in every field of the state, political, economic, social and cultural life. The Constitution ensures that the state will provide for mothers and children, protect pregnant women, give maternity leave, develop maternity clinics, nurseries and pre-schools. It also ensures women equality in the job market, in education and professional careers. It guarantees the right of equal pay for equal work, the right to rest and leisure, to social security, to dignity, to decorations and to occupy posts of higher rank.

The NGOs Committee believes that the amended 1952 constitution approaches the problem of gender equality in the paternalistic way. Indeed, the statement that women are granted equal rights to men takes men as the point of departure, and is itself discriminatory. The new Constitution, may address some of those issues: the draft provision prohibiting discrimination includes the more neutral wording 'on the basis of … sex'. The list also includes a provision banning discrimination on the basis of sexual orientation.

The Labour Code contains a number of provisions regulating women's employment, with the declared intention of protecting women from an officially perceived risk to their health and reproductive functions and helping them reconcile employment with maternity and homemaking duties. However, there is no similar requirement for men to reconcile their work with domestic responsibilities. Women's earnings have been, on average, 30 per cent lower than men's and women over thirty-five years of age face extremely limited employment opportunities. The list of professions from which women are excluded, on the pretext of protecting their health, comprises over ninety occupations in twenty fields of employment. Women's retirement age is set at sixty, men's at sixty-five. In practice, this often means compulsory retirement, although the Constitutional Tribunal has ruled that making such retirement mandatory is discriminatory; even so, women who live longer than men often spend their last years deep in poverty as a result.

The qualifying age for marriage is eighteen for women while it is twenty-one for men (a court can approve lower respective limits of sixteen and eighteen). Divorce is finalized once a court determines that the marriage has irretrievably disintegrated – requiring detailed often humiliating, testimony by the spouses – and can be denied if the court decides it would harm the children, 'principles of community life' or if divorce is sought by the spouse who is exclusively guilty of the marriage breakdown.

RLG has not reported instances of the denial of custodial rights to lesbian women per se. However, it does note that when a biological mother dies, her lesbian partner is denied custodial rights over the children. Some right-wing politicians have issued statements that they would seek to extend the current ban on the adoption of children by homosexuals to deny homosexual biological parents from custody rights.

The 1993 Law on Family Planning, Foetus Protection and Conditions on Admissibility of Abortion forbids women from terminating pregnancy on social grounds; abortion is permitted in the case of rape, incest or severe deformity of the foetus. While women who undergo illegal abortions are not prosecuted, the doctors performing the abortion and anyone seen to assist – whether financially or by other means, including trips to foreign countries – may be held criminally responsible and face imprisonment. While the law mandates sex education and the availability of contraceptives, the sex education curriculum is still unwritten (and is deeply controversial); buyers of contraceptives complain that their purchases are not kept confidential by pharmacies, especially in smaller communities.

Insemination, adoption and fostering

AI clinics operate in a legal grey area, according to reports in the English-language weekly *Warsaw Voice*. The Warsaw prosecutor closed one clinic down on the grounds that it violated the 1993 anti-abortion law (since embryos are stored and disposed of), but it was reopened when the Minister of Health intervened. There have been no reports of lesbians seeking to use the services of insemination clinics.

The law forbids payment to either parents or intermediaries by adoptive parents. RLG reports that courts routinely exclude homosexual people from approval as adoptive parents.

Women have the right to paid maternity leave – sixteen weeks for the first birth, eighteen weeks for the next birth(s) and twenty-six weeks for a multiple birth. Women who have taken on foster children or have filed with the guardianship court receive the same benefits.

Child and family benefits, childcare

Unpaid childcare leave may be granted for three years (with another three if the child has a chronic illness or disability requiring special parental care). If the mother needs childcare benefits because of insufficient means of support during unpaid leave (where the family income per person is less than 25 per cent of the average monthly income in the state sector), she may obtain a sum equivalent to twenty-four months of her previous pay for one child or thirty-six months if she is single or if there is a multiple birth.

The future

Political commentary on the new Constitution's proposed anti-discrimination clause indicates that even supporters will not interpret the provision as providing legal protection to same-sex partnerships. Homosexual rights groups have launched public discussion about legalizing partnerships, but the debate has yet to enter the political arena. Similarly, women's rights organizations have been leading public debate to make legislation on family matters, domestic violence and rape more equitable. Social security benefits are to be restructured in the coming years; Parliament will probably not take up the issue until late 1996, and it is unknown how or whether benefits to mothers will be affected.

Support groups

The following women's rights organizations are nationwide groups based in Warsaw that are supportive on questions of lesbian rights. They were among the leaders of the 12 organizations making up the Polish NGOs Committee for the Beijing 1995 delegation. Telephones are usually answered during business hours on weekdays.

Women's Rights Centre, Tel: 48 22 620 76 24
Centre for the Advancement of Women, Tel: 48 22 629 92 58
Polish Feminist Association, Tel: 48 22 628 87 63

National Lesbian Archives
c/o Olga Stefanuik
v. Sukiennicza 7m 70
PL–91851 Lodz
Tel/Fax: 48 42 578262

At the time of writing, Poland's only nationwide homosexual rights group, Lambda, is in the throes of major structural change, as it converts from a national organization with local chapters into a national network of independently registered local groups; as a result, some contact addresses below may change or disappear. Local homosexual rights groups also operate in Warsaw and Olsztyn. Most groups have lesbian members and declare themselves to be open to working on lesbian-specific topics, but as yet no lesbian-specific organizations are operating in Poland. Lambda Warszawa, the national organization's Warsaw chapter, has a telephone help-line which lesbian mothers operate on Wednesdays.

Homosexual rights groups in Poland include:

Lambda Warszawa
c/o Universytet Warszawski
ul. Krakowskie Przedmiescie 24 00-071
Warszawa
Lambda's Warsaw address is ONLY a mailing address. It also serves as the national Lambda address. If you wish to contact the national organization, address your correspondence to S.G. Lambda instead of 'Lambda Warszawa'.
Lambda Warszawa Rainbow Centre telephone helpline:48 22 628 52 22 (operates 18:00 to 21:00 on the following evenings: Wed., lesbian; Fri. general, primarily gay; Tues., lesbian and gay Christians)

Some other Lambda affiliates:

Inicjatywa Gdanska,
skr poczt 34,
80-250 Gdansk 44

Lambda Krakow,
skr. poczt 249,
30-960 Krakow 1

Lambda Poznan,
skr. poczt 176,
60-959 Poznan;
Tel: 48 61 53 76 55
Fri. 17:00–21:00

Ruch Lesbeijk i Gejow (RLG),
skr. poczt. 63, 00-405 Warszawa 15
Tel: 48 22 628 03 36
Fri. 17:00–20:00
Stowarzyszenie Tolersex,
Warsaw (no address available);
helpline 48 22 635 54 67
Fri. 18:00-21:00

Nieformalna Grupa Lambola Olsztyn
skr. poczt. 377
10-959 Olsztyn 2

Portugal

ADELAIDE PENHA e COSTA

Compiled September 1995

Statistical overview

Source: *CIRCA*

Capital: Lisbon
Population: 9,800,000 (1994)
Language: Portuguese
Religions: Roman Catholic 97%, Protestant 1%, other (including Muslim and Jewish) 2%.
Divorces: 10,649 (1991)
Births: 12 per 1000 (1993)
Deaths: 11 per 1000 (1993)
Life expectancy: 78.9 for women, 72.1 for men (1994)
Infant mortality: 9 per 1000 (1992)

General climate and indicators

There is a strenuous effort on the part of all party political forces in Portugal to endorse the nuclear heterosexual family. Despite moves even in neighbouring Spain towards a recognition of alternative family types such as registered partnerships, and the example of countries like Denmark that recognize same-sex marriages, in profoundly Catholic Portugal there is no hint of such developments.

Before 1991, lesbians were largely invisible, then several popular women's magazines, ran articles on lesbianism, often featuring foreign figures such as Vita Sackville West and Virginia Woolf. Lately, however, in the middle-market magazine *Mulher Moderna*, a considerable amount of attention has been given to ordinary

Portuguese lesbians. The interviewees are always anonymous or given assumed names, as is the case on extremely rare occasions when lesbians have appeared on television. This is as much for their own protection as for any other reason.

There is only one lesbian association in Portugal, the magazine *Lilas*, and even its production staff use pseudonyms or just first names. One of them, a teacher, has been quite clearly warned not to bring her 'lifestyle' to work.

Popular attitudes towards lesbianism, where they exist, range from the celebration in the more liberal press of 'lesbian chic' to photographs of Gay Pride parades from other countries, accompanied by condemnatory captions, to outright hostility, as when a recent poll elected 'homosexuals' as the third most disliked category of neighbour.

Legislation

It is customary to say that there is no anti-lesbian or gay legislation in Portugal. This is not true. The area of the civil code dealing with marriage considers several types of marriage as invalid. As regards same-sex unions, these are considered non-existent, because such unions cannot by their very nature be included within the 'relation of complementarity ... which is based on the difference between the two sexes'. There is therefore a significant difference between the 1975 law and the first, albeit naïve stirrings of 'acceptance' in some women's magazines.

Then there are laws regulating 'public morals and public decency'. Fortunately these are sufficiently vague and sufficiently appalling to most reasonable judicial minds not to be a real danger to any lesbian whose sexuality is exposed in a court of law.

There is no legislation providing for lesbian rights of any kind, which reflects the prevailing view that such women do not exist in Portugal. There are of course lesbians in Portugal, some of whom occupy high places in public life, including political and government circles. However, they are all heavily closeted and do nothing for lesbian rights.

This combination of invisibility, a high profile when there is the very occasional need to punish, and the vagaries of judges' minds in interpreting 'decency,' means that lesbians live intersticial existences, fearful of discovery, and the subsequent loss of family ties and jobs.

Custody is not a foregone conclusion for lesbian mothers, although it seems to be a fact that most fathers do not want custody of the children and very often give up their accorded visiting hours, days, weekends and holidays. However, it is also clear that when the father is interested in claiming his share of the children's time, the lesbian mother who has a lesbian partner faces great difficulties in negotiating suitable arrangements.

During divorce proceedings, lesbian mothers feel the overwhelming need to disguise and hide their lesbianism. If the husband should introduce evidence of his wife's lesbianism, the issue then becomes, not custody, but the sexual orientation of the woman. This often gives rise to the most retrograde and homophobic discussions. On the other hand, courts do not always take seriously a husband's accusation of lesbianism against his wife, as the word 'lesbian' is frequently used as an insult.

Illegitimacy does not exist in Portugal: a woman is forced to disclose the father's identity, who then, regardless of the wishes of the mother, has rights over the child.

Insemination, adoption and fostering

Insemination is difficult for heterosexual couples. I do not for one moment imagine that it would be easier for lesbians. Single women have been known, in special circumstances, to be allowed to adopt children; and this probably remains a lesbian couple's best option – if one of them acted individually, i.e. as a single woman.

The future

I have no idea when we are going to emerge from this morass. I myself am involved in *Lilas* and we are doing our best.

Support groups

Lilas is a quarterly lesbian magazine, the only exclusively lesbian magazine currently published in Portugal. We are a collective of six lesbians and have been publishing for three years. We have published texts on lesbian history, introducing prominent lesbians, theoretical texts on lesbianism and feminism, texts on the lesbian present (analyses of the current situation in Portugal), coming-out stories and other texts which bear witness to lesbian lives in Portugal, and book and film reviews. The magazine also has a 'news in brief' section.

Our main aim might be described as the casting of a lesbian gaze on the reality that surrounds us, with an emphasis on how lesbians see themselves and on those who look at us. We also aim at enhancing lesbians self-esteem, which is on the whole rather low in this country.

Lilas
Apartado 6104
2700 Amadora

Russia

MASHA GESSEN

Compiled March 1996

Statistical overview

Source: Institute of Social and Economic Issues of the Population

Capital: Moscow
Population: 147,000,000 (1994)
Languages: Russian is the language of administration and ecommuni-cation, although hundreds of other languages are spoken.
Religions: Russian Orthodox is the largest denomination. There is a sig-nificant Muslim minority and various small groups practising other religions.
Marriages: 7.5 per 1000 (1993)
Divorces: 4.5 per 1000 or 600 per 1,000 marriages (1993)
Births: 9.7 (1994)
Deaths: 14.5 (1993)
Infant mortality: 19.9 (1993)
Life expectancy: 71.9 for women, 58.9 for men (1993)
Single mothers/households headed by women: 40% of all households have a woman as their main breadwinner; every fifth baby is born outside of marriage.

General climate and indicators

Official persecution of lesbians and gay men in Russia took root in the systematic obliteration of privacy and individuality undertaken by the Soviets. So-called 'revolutionary morality' moved the Bolsheviks in 1918 to abolish the family as Russia had known it. The ban on homo-sexuality that had existed in pre-revolutionary Russia had already been abolished, along with the rest of the laws of the empire, in 1917. But it seems that what was motivating the makers of the new morality was less a precursor to free love than a desire to subjugate individual will, belief and desire to a new general policy: whatever was useful to the revolution and in the interests of the proletarian class struggle was moral; whatever was harmful to it was immoral and intolerable.

In the realm of personal life, this process of subjugation took a para-doxical form. A Family and Marriage Code adopted in 1926 made reg-istration unnecessary for the recognition of marriage and made divorce a mere (and inexpensive) formality. The aim of the law was to abolish all ties between individuals, leaving each isolated in relation to the state. Just ten years later, the state acted to tighten the marriage bonds it had itself loosened, creating a new family unit to replace the one that had been destroyed. Divorce was made much more difficult under the 1936 Family and Marriage Code. Abortion, legal since 1920, was also banned in 1936. New rhetoric declared the family an impor-tant unit of the collective. But the restoration of the family – with the state itself as an additional member – had begun even earlier, evi-denced in the law of 8 June, 1934, that made 'betrayal of the homeland' punishable by death and made all members of a 'traitor's' family col-lectively responsible for his or her deed.

Thus the lives of heterosexuals became legislated, their privacy obliterated and their individuality usurped by the state. Those who fell ouside the heterosexual units that had become the building blocks of the new state faced persecution.

Since the early 1930s, when the Soviet government began its long-term anti-homosexual witch-hunt, the psychiatric institutions have posed the greatest threat to lesbians. The professional provisions that compel psychiatrists to treat lesbians have remained unchanged, and until a new law was passed in 1992, it was exceedingly easy to com-mit someone to a psychiatric institution. This law still does not protect the most vulnerable group of lesbians: young women who have not reached legal majority and continue to be legally in the guardianship of their elders.

Until 1990, lesbian networks in Russia – the only ways for lesbians to make contact with one another – were informal and largely closed (newcomers could not be trusted, and the fear of persecution was too great to take risks). Now there are more formal lesbian organizations in Moscow, St Petersburg, and the Siberian cities of Omsk and Novosibirsk. None of these groups, however, are formally recognized by the government. The organizers report that the people who come to these networks suffer from intense loneliness, often having never met other lesbians.

For most of the century Moscow has been concerned about the low birth rate (especially for ethnic Russians), so various legislative and social measures were introduced to encourage women to have children. For example, single mothers – women who have children out of wedlock, not widowed or divorced mothers – are granted additional state benefits. One beneficial government action succeeded was the removal of the stigma of single parenthood: today 40 per cent of babies are born out of wedlock.

The belief that motherhood is the proper function of woman has not been challenged in this society. Most first children are born to women under twenty. Like other women, many lesbians have children quite young, often before they come out as lesbians. Because motherhood is taken as the natural way of things, there is rarely conflict between it and a woman's identity as a lesbian. Conversely, few women identify explicitly as lesbian mothers: they are women – hence, mothers – and also lesbians.

Legislation

Lesbian sex has never been criminalized in Russia and lesbian motherhood is not regulated by any laws.

The Family Code, signed into law on 29 December, 1995, does not specify what a court should consider in custody decisions. At the same time, the law makes it clear that all rights and responsibilities regarding children stem from biological parenthood. When a birth is registered, a father may not necessarily be indicated, though if the woman was married within ten months preceding the birth, her husband will be assumed to be the child's father. In practice, in over 90 per cent of cases custody is awarded to the mother. Parental rights can be limited by court decision at the request of the police, law enforcement agencies, guardianship agencies, the other parent or close relatives of the child. To limit parental rights a court must hold that being with the parent is dangerous for the child. The law does not define 'dangerous'.

Though there have not been any widely publicized cases of mothers losing custody because of their lesbianism, many lesbian mothers believe this is exactly what would happen if their sexual identity became known. They tend to remain closeted and to broker custody agreements with the fathers of their children without going to court.

Insemination, adoption and fostering

There is no law regulating insemination. During the discussion of the new Family Code in 1995, the Duma (lower house of Parliament) considered introducing a ban on AI for lesbians. This proposal was rejected.

Two people who are not married cannot adopt a child together, though single people can adopt. There is nothing in the law that should prevent a lesbian from adopting her partner's child if the mother consents. Still, it seems unlikely this would happen, since adoption is granted by a court on the recommendation of the local guardianship agency. Guardians may be appointed only to children who do not have parents who serve as guardians. The law specifies that in appointing guardians, the court has to consider the 'moral and other qualities' of the applicant, which would seem to exclude lesbians. In appointing a foster family, the court is obligated to consider the opinion of the child; a child over ten years of age has to give her or his consent. A child could conceivably insist on being placed with lesbians.

Child and family benefits, childcare

Family and labour laws provide an impressive set of benefits for mothers and families with children. Since the beginning of the 1990s, however, most of these benefits have in reality become negligible. For example, laws provide for a parental leave of up to three years after the birth of the baby, with partial salary compensation and a guaranteed job to return to. But because many companies are going out of business, the job guarantee is effectively worthless; other employers easily violate the provision, because it lacks an enforcement mechanism. Similarly, though the law provides for employer-subsidized childcare, free pre-school care has become a thing of the past.

A man who was married to the mother of a child at or just before birth, or who is indicated on the birth certificate as the child's father (this requires the man's consent), or who is determined by a court to be the child's father (courts may consider witness testimony or blood tests as evidence) will generally be ordered to pay alimony. The father's employer is responsible for collecting alimony out of his salary. But because of low official salaries and the prevalence of hidden employment, alimony too has become largely meaningless.

The future

The birth rate in Russia is going down, the economic conditions are difficult and state support structures have all but collapsed. Lesbians, like other women, are likely to think twice about having children.

Triangle, the Moscow-based lesbian and gay organization, regularly publishes articles about lesbian motherhood in its bulletin, and started organizing a series of seminars for lesbian mothers in December 1995. Although the original aim was to develop a support group for lesbian mothers, the group soon opened up to all lesbians.

Support group

Triangle, the Russian association of gays, lesbians and bisexuals, Moscow

Tel/Fax: 7 095 163 8002
Tel: 7 095 166 2418
e-mail: triangle@glas.apc.org

Serbia

LISA A. MULHOLLAND
Compiled March 1996

Efforts to find a single profile writer for Serbia did not meet with success.

Instead, the following is compiled from information gathered from the *World Atlas* 1995, *Etat Du Monde* 1996, a report for an ILGA conference in 1993 by Lepa Mladjenovic and Zeljko Radovanac of Arkadija, e-mail responses from Lepa Mladjenovic in February and March of 1996, her essay 'Where I Come From' in *Lola Press* (1994) and the *Report on Lesbians in Yugoslavia* by Jelica Todosijevic of Arkadija Lesbian Working Group, distributed by e-mail in March 1995.

Statistical overview

Source: see above

Capital: Belgrade
Population: 10,850,000 (1994)
Languages: Serbo-Croat, Albanian in Kosova, Hungarian in Vojvodina
Ethnic groups: 60% Serbian, 20% Albanian 10% Hungarians, Romas (Gypsies), Romanians, and Muslims.
Religion: Christian
Infant mortality: 19.6 (1993)
Life expectancy: 75.3 for women, 70.3 for men (1994)

General climate and indicators

Following the cessation of war, the entire region of former Yugoslavia is undergoing a significant period of transition. Arkadija, Belgrade's gay and lesbian group, reports frequent political and physical attacks against open homosexuals, mainly gay men in known gathering spots. Lesbians remain invisible in society, often leading double lives: displaying a public face in a heterosexual family, while conducting private life with a girlfriend or woman lover. Few of these women identify with the word 'lesbian' according to Lepa Mladjenovic, an activist working with Arkadija, preferring instead to see themselves as 'human beings in love with a person'. In February of 1996, Mladjenovic wrote the following:

> I don't know one woman who lives with a woman and children who wants to talk about it. Not one of the few I know ever told their children that they are with women. Most do not use the word lesbian nor do they use co-mothering as a term.

Jelica Todosijevic is also an activist with Arkadija. In her March 1995 report she explained that a woman's value is determined by the man she lives with or is married to. Single women and lesbians, therefore, have lower value in the society and as Jelica points out have less access to everything from decent housing to working wages.

A street survey conducted in 1994 by Arkadija found that citizens of Belgrade apparently view lesbianism as an illness.

On 5 May 1995, lesbian members of Arkadija were attacked in the street as they were spray-painting graffiti and being filmed by a Canadian crew documenting lesbian life in eastern Europe.

Legislation

In July 1994 a new criminal law was accepted in Serbia, decriminalizing male homosexuality.

Although lesbianism is not mentioned explicitly in family law, mothers are afraid to have their homosexuality brought up in court, as it can be used to take custody away from them. Given that lesbians are seen to belong to the same category as those who are 'irresponsibly promiscuous, equal to a drug addict or mentally disturbed and dangerous', according to Todosijevic, judges are not likely to make a decision in their favour.

Arkadija members are planning actions around the issue of registered partnership, wrote Mladjenovic in a letter of March 1996:

Our law expert wanted to write the scientific paper for the national congress of criminologists about the need and the situation of partnership lists and lesbian and gay marriage in Europe, with the suggestion to propose such a law in this country. One professor, a woman lawyer disqualified this paper proposal for presentation at the congress last week, saying 'enough of this feminism'.

Insemination, adoption and fostering

According to Mladjenovic (March 1996), there are new private clinics operating for those who can afford them. Single women can be inseminated and so, theoretically, can lesbians. No lesbian is yet known to have been impregnated via these clinics.

Adoption is normally restricted to heterosexual couples. A few, well-connected single women have been allowed to adopt, but no known lesbian has been successful.

The future

The country is torn by the brutality of war. Returning soldiers are violent, and 'others' be they homosexual, foreign, feminist, or pacifist, are targets for abuse. Women in general are also victimized, again valued more for their biological reproductive capacity or sexual services than their humanity.

Mladjenovic, in her February 1996 letter, explained that Arkadija has never highlighted the issue of lesbian families, nor do they have any women willing to speak publicly about their situation. One recent request by a female television journalist was denied by Mladjenovic after it became clear the journalist was in search of 'sensation' rather than a responsible discussion.

On 8 March 1996 lesbians participated in the International Women's Day demonstration 'For Womens Rights' on the streets of Belgrade and distributed a leaflet with the title, 'Lesbian Rights Are Women's Rights - Women's Rights Are Human Rights'. Labris members are are now planning to work on the first book on lesbian lives in the former Yugoslavia which, writes Mladjenovic, will be 'a book that lesbians and heterosexuals should be proud of'.

Support groups

Labris, the lesbian working group within Arkadija, meets weekly to organize workshops dealing with issues central to lesbian life.

Labris/Arkadija
c/o Zenski Centar
Tirsova 5a 11000
Beograd
Contact tel: 381.11.687.190
e-mail: zenski_centar@zamir-bg.ztn.apc.org

Slovakia
HANNAH WOLFSON
Compiled April 1996

Statistical overview

Source: State Office of Statistics

Capital: Bratislava
Population: 5,336,455 (1993); 51% female
Language: State language is Slovak
Ethnic groups: 85% Slovak, 10% Hungarian, 1.5% Romany, 1% Czech, Moravian and Silesian, 0.6% Ruthenian and Ukrainian
Religions: 60% Roman Catholic, 18% unknown, 10% without denomination, 6% Lutheran, 3% Greek Catholic, 2% Protestant
Marriages: 5.8 per 1000 inhabitants

49% of women are married, 49% of men

38% women are single, 47% men

4% women are divorced, 3% men

11% women widowed, 2% men

Divorces: 1.6 per 1000
Births: 13.8 per 1000

1.96 children per woman

Deaths: 9.9 per 1000
Infant mortality: 10.6 deaths up to one year, per 1000 births

perinatal mortality: 9.3 per 1000

neonatal mortality: 7.1 per 1000

Life expectancy: 73 for women, 63 for men
Single mothers/households headed by women: 159,133

General climate and indicators

Sitting at a small gathering of a women's magazine in Bratislava, K. smiled at the idea of lesbian motherhood in Slovakia. 'That is not the problem', she said. 'The hard part is being a single mother here.'

K., the mother of a four-year-old, is struggling with single mother-hood in a country where less than 10 per cent of the population remains unmarried, alternative partnerships are rarely found and the divorce rate in 1990, the first year after the collapse of socialism was just 1.6 per 1,000. Not only that, she and all the other women, lesbian or heterosexual, are trying to make it on their own in a society that lays two very heavy burdens on women.

On the one hand, Socialist Czechoslovakia did a great deal for women. The 1969 Constitution promised equal opportunities for men and women within the family, the workplace and public life. In 1980, women made up 44.6 per cent of the workforce, the state provided guaranteed maternity leave of three years and an extensive and free kindergarten system. Both technical schools and universities encour-aged women to take advantage of the state-funded education system, in fact, today, half of all university graduates are women.

On the other hand, however, the traditional Slovak lifestyle never receded into the background. A strongly Catholic society and a pre-dominantly rural population ensured that women continued to marry and have children young. While it was taken for granted that a woman would work and contribute financially, it was also assumed that she would value family life above all else. Family still remains the central focus for Slovak women: a survey conducted by the Fokus Agency in 1995 found that marriage and family receive the highest status in public opinion. Indeed, Slovakia has one of the highest mar-riage rates in Europe: according to the survey, the majority of adults get married at least once, and only 10 per cent of women over the age of twenty are unmarried.

Not only are women expected to marry, they are expected to do so when young. Ninety-six per cent of Slovaks say a woman should be married by the age of twenty-five; 71 per cent expect them to have married by the age of twenty-three and 44 per cent by the age of twenty-one. And reality is closely in line with the expectations: the average age is twenty-one, and that number has been dropping gradually since the mid-1980s. And while the Slovak opinion towards sex is fairly open – 70 per cent of the population has no problems with premarital sex – the vast majority of children are born to married women. In 1994, only 12 per cent of children were born out of wedlock; even more striking, 45 per cent of Slovak women marry because they are pregnant, and almost half of the first children are born fewer than nine months after marriage.

And what about those few who choose to remain unmarried? They are open to the same discrimination that women with traditional families face, especially the assumption from managers, both male and female, that they will abandon their employer before the age of twenty-five to dedicate themselves to having children. In addition, they face poverty: because women make on average almost one-third less than men, it is a struggle to support a family on a single woman's salary. They also face society's suspicions about the motives of independent women. In fact, according to the Fokus poll, 24 per cent of Slovaks openly admit that they have a highly negative view of 'feminism', characterizing women who call themselves feminists as anything from angry radical, to deranged amazon lesbians. All in all, it is not an easy atmosphere in which to function.

The public's perception of lesbianism is hard to gauge, especially since very few people talk openly about homosexuality. The strong Church presence guarantees that most Slovaks, particularly the older, less educated rural population view homosexual life as anathema. The Fokus survey asked people to evaluate the attention that should be devoted to addressing adult issues in schools: 51 per cent of respondents said that schools should pay little attention to questions of homosexuality.

According to Anka Falryova, a writer for the feminist literary magazine Aspect and the founder of the lesbian support group Museion, there are about a dozen lesbian mothers spread throughout Slovakia.

Museion conducts its business via the postal system, and Falryova regularly answers letters from lesbian women across the country. That is all she can do, she says, because it is virtually impossible to persuade Slovak lesbians to come out or to establish personal contact. In fact, many find even accepting their own sexuality too much of an obstacle to overcome. Falryova tells the story of one woman in a small town in central Slovakia who wrote to Museion asking for help. After Falryova's response, the woman wrote once more, to say that she had been to church, that she could not face that fact that she was lesbian and therefore evil, and Museion should not contact her further. The scenario, Falryova said, is a common one, and she often wonders if her own work is at all helpful. Until Slovakia's attitudes about homosexuality become more open, she fears it is just a matter of helping women to be strong, and waiting.

In a recent letter, the Museion Stred group organizers wrote:

It is very hard to tell you anything about the life of lesbians in Slovakia (let alone lesbian mothers) because they live hidden lives. There are only around one hundred addresses known in the whole country. We know only two mothers; one of them is divorced on the grounds of her homosexuality (very unusual here) and the other one is still married (her husband knows but wants to keep the family together).

Slovak society is very conservative, everything that doesn't match the ideal of a 'normal' family (man, woman, kids) is regarded as deviant and bad. Not only the pressure of this society makes people choose such a life (probably most lesbians choose this), also the financial situation makes it hard to raise a family by yourself.

Looking at the situation for lesbians and lesbian mothers, it can be said that it is hard to survive openly in this country, because society does not tolerate the phenomena at all. Living openly as a lesbian can bring a person great problems, because there is a very big chance of losing your job. Furthermore neighbours and other people around can make life very unpleasant. Children of openly lesbian mothers would have a very hard time surviving in school.

Considering the fact that the society is still so very conservative, it is not surprising that there is no legal basis for this group; same-sex partnership cannot be registered (although we keep fighting for it at the ministry), insemination, adoption and fostering are out of the question and there is hardly any help available.

The work of our organization is limited alot; it is hard to find financial support; publication in normal magazines and newspapers is very hard, the same goes for finding more lesbians and help outside our group; and normal living (even if it is hidden) is hard — officially for two women who are not related living together, etc. ... Changes for the better will go slowly, but the younger generation gives us hope for improvement. In towns the situation is a bit better than in the villages (more progressive influences and the possibilty of relative anonymity).'

Legislation

There are no laws directly governing homosexuality in Slovakia. Unsurpisingly, there is no standard registration of same-sex partnerships.

Insemination, adoption and fostering

There is little available information on adoption, suffice it to say that it is extremely rare and most orphaned or abandoned children remain in children's homes.

Child and family benefits, childcare

Although the state paternalism of the socialist era is fading into the background, there is still a very solid network of social services. Slovaks still have access to free health care, and there is a special network of local gynaecological clinics for pregnant women. Current labour laws also provide for three years of unpaid maternity leave, with a requirement that employers must guarantee the woman her position when she returns. However, there is a government proposal, currently in still in draft form, to change the length of leave to five years. According to Jarmila Janŏsová, President of the Women's Council of the Confederation of Labour Unions, the goal of the plan is not only to change the leave time but also to weaken the requirements placed on employers.

Education is free and compulsory, and begins at a young age. The Education Act of 1990 guarantees free access to daycare for children from the age of six months to three years (creches), and to kindergartens for children aged two to six. However, in 1991, responsibility for the creches was transferred from the state government to local administrations, and many closed. The report from the Ministries of Foreign Affairs and Labour, Social Affairs and the Family to the United Nations Commission on the Status of Women predicts that it is likely that the number of childcare facilities will continue to be reduced in an effort to encourage mothers to stay at home for all three years of maternity leave.

The future

Life in the gay and lesbian community is opening up, albeit very slowly. Yes, Slovakia is a very Catholic country, but even the Church is helping out in eastern Slovakia, cooperating with Ganymedes, the gay men's support network, to set up a hotline and two discussion groups to enable homosexual seminarians to talk to each other.

The best place to be, though, is Bratislava, the capital city. The city's first gay restaurant opened recently, and small support groups are starting to gather. Lesbians as well are starting to become more visible, although an expatriate lesbian couple complained that it is still difficult to make contact with lesbians outside of the student population.

In terms of the future of lesbian motherhood in Slovakia, any advance will require changes in the public's attitude about single motherhood and about the role of women in general. Unfortunately, even women involved in the feminist movement seem unsure of what to do to make life easier for women, because the issues at hand are not tied up in easily approachable problems like a lack of education, inadequate health care or a ban on women in the workplace. Instead, Slovakia's attitude towards women originates from a tradition many, many years old.

Support groups

Museion
PO Box 122
814 99 Bratislava

Museion Stred (in Central Slovakia)
PO Box 410
974 01 Banska Bystrica

Museion also has a junior section for teenagers.

███

Slovenia

ALENKA A. PUHAR

Compiled May 1995

Statistical overview

Source: State Office of Statistics

Capital: Ljubljana

Language: Slovene

Ethnic groups: predominantly Slovene with Italian and Hungarian minorities and a large number of immigrants from former Yugoslavia (officially 30,000 but actual number much higher)

Religion: Roman Catholic

Marriages: 4.5 per 1000 (1993), decreasing, 6.5 per 1000 (1983)

Divorces: 2.17 per 1000 (1993)

Births: 7.1 per 1000, 1.31 per 1000 live births

     19,793 live births, 95 stillborn

     28% out of wedlock (1993)

Deaths: 20,012 (1993)

Infant mortality: 6.6 per 1000 live births (1993)

Life expectancy: 75.3 for women, 68 for men

All these data refer to the *de iure* population, i.e. the citizens of Slovenia and its permanent residents. As there are many refugees from the rest of Yugoslavia in the country – the official number is 30,000, but their actual number is much higher – and as the majority of them are women with children, the number of single mothers is bound to be higher, although many of them do not possess a household to head.

General climate and indicators

It is difficult to describe uch private phenomena as sexual lives and habits. The best starting point would seem to be an examination of some of the common cliches. It has been a customary to present the Communist countries as extremely puritanical, narrow-minded and conformist, while the period of transition to democracy has been described in two simplistic and astonishingly disparate ways: first, as a period towards liberation, second, as a period of growing religious-ness and the increased power of the Church.

Since the early years of the 1990s, Yugoslavia has apparently shed this puritanical image. Bookshops, libraries and newsstands were full of various literature, the movies were only occasionally edited, nudist camps proliferated. At the same time various less visible, but more important changes were happening: in the early 1960s, for instance, so-called sexual education was introduced in the elementary and high school curricula and contraceptives became available, regardless of marital status, although abortion (legal and free of charge) remained a popular method of contraception. During this period, illegitimacy lost most of its stigma, at least in Slovenia, as a growing number of women decided to have a child but not to marry.

On the other hand, homosexuality, male or female, remained a sub-ject of embarrassment, something that was not discussed freely in public. It had been, of course, the subject of debate in the 1970s, when the new and more modern family legislation was being prepared. The result was the decriminalization of homosexuality in 1977, in Slovenia and Croatia (but not in the remaining republics of Yugoslavia). As important as the step was, it has to be stressed that the law only fol-lowed the practice. There are no records (or memories) of any cases of prosecution for the past forty years. (The early post-war years could prove different, but I was not able to find any reliable data or research on the subject.) The police limited its intervention to the cases of vio-lence against or among homosexuals.

If the former regime cannot be described as very puritanical, the behaviour of heterosexual people cannot be described as 'provoca-tive', outspoken or assertive. The situation can best be described as moderate on both sides. In Yugoslavia, and in Slovenia, the 1960s had been a period of liberalization, both political and cultural as well as sexual, but gay communities were not established and did not openly defy the regime or the prejudices. This, however, changed in the 1980s.

In this regard Slovenia differed radically from the rest of the communist countries of eastern Europe. The 1980s saw the emergence of various alternative, dissident and protest movements, in which the struggle for sexual nonconformity was very much an integral part. Gay and lesbian activities gradually increased, culminating in 1984 with an international homosexual festival in Ljubljana. The event was highly controversial. The authorities condemned it and tried to stop it, while the general population – or at least its most vocal part – was in favour. The festival subsequently became an annual event and celebrated its tenth anniversary in 1994.

The event caused far greater uproar in the rest of Yugoslavia and helped, in an interesting way, in the dissolution of the country. It served to establish (or reinforce) some stereotypes which soon entered the political battlefield. In the eyes of most of Yugoslavia, Slovenia became a country of gays – rich and spoiled, degenerate, decadent, sinful, infested with AIDS, its Communist authorities powerless to restore order or punish the rebellious adolescents. On the other hand, the rest of the country, which was predominantly Serbian, fostered a macho image, proud of their fighting tradition as tough and invincible warriors. There is a rich verbal and visual treasure (for example, cartoons and magazine covers) to illustrate how the process of democratization was felt and seen as a sexual relationship, a marital fight, that gradually led to the actual war in 1991. The fighting, (which in Slovenia lasted for ten days only) was again described in unmistakable sexual terms: as an orgy, a rape, a duel between feminine and masculine partners.

To go back to the issue of homosexual activism: from the early 1980s on, gay and lesbian clubs, groups and activities became a more or less accepted part of life in Slovenia. Prominent groups have included Magnus (male homosexuals) and Lilith or LL (lesbians); the Roza Klub and Roza Disco (roza translates as pink), Project Plus and AIDS fond, magazines *Revolver* and *Keke(c)* (mixed) and *Pandora* (lesbian), several bulletins and a publishing house, Lambda. They gained their official status under the cover of youth or student organizations, (as independent forms of organized activities were illegal), and shared their premises, finances, etc. Most of these events were described as 'firsts' in the eastern half of Europe. The statement that 'nowhere in the region of Eastern Europe there existed an openly gay bar or cafe before 1989' is not quite true as it leaves out Slovenia.

Legislation

The problem of homosexual marriages was first officially recognized and publicized in 1988, when a proposal, submitted by a group of homosexuals, in favour of same-sex marriages was endorsed at the Congress of Socialist Youth of Slovenia (the official youth organization). This led to the formation in 1992 of Yoldoshimm a group of homosexual couples whose goal is the legalization of same-sex marriages.

But the issue really took off in 1992 when a male couple (with a history of ten years of stable cohabitation) wrote and published a demand for the legalization of same-sex marriages. It was referred to the Constitutional Court, which examined the issue of the unconstitutionality of the existing family legislation. At the time of writing, the Court is still researching the issue. Some political parties are in favour of the reform and an official project on necessary legal changes was made in the Office for Women's Policy (attached to the government). The range of proposed reforms is wide and includes, for instance, the right of asylum for foreign citizens, in cases of persecution because of sexual orientation. The move was accompanied by an appeal backed by many prominent men and women. Public opinion is quite clear: some polls have shown that at least a third of the population is in favour of same-sex marriages.

In cases of divorce, children are mostly put into their mother's custody (in more than 90 per cent of cases). Single parenthood is considered a normal feature of modern life and there is no legal discrimination.

Child and family benefits, childcare

Medical care during pregnancy, maternity leave (11 months) and similar benefits are liberal and non-discriminatory.

Insemination, adoption and fostering

AI is available for single as well as married women.

Support group

LL Group
Kersnikova
4 SL-61000 Ljubljana
Tel: 386 61 132 40 89

Spain

PERE CRUELLS

Compiled February 1996

Statistical overview

Source: *CIRCA*

Capital: Madrid
Population: 39,600,000 (1994)
Languages: Castilian (Spanish). The main regional languages (Catalan, Basque and Galician) are also official in their locality.
Catalan (64% in Catalonia, 71% in Balearics, 49% in the Valencian region)
Basque (25% in the Basque region), Galician (90% in Galicia)
Religions: Roman Catholic 96%, other (including Protestant, Jewish, Muslim) 4%
Divorces: 23,063 (1991)
Births: 10 per 1000 (1993)
Deaths: 9 per 1000 (1993)
Life expectancy: 81.0 for women, 75.3 for men (1994)
Infant mortality: 8 per 1000 (1992)

General climate and indicators

Although Spain is a Catholic country, with a supposedly narrow mind about subjects such as homosexuality, public opinion is very permissive. Nowadays very few people have aggressive or discriminatory attitudes towards gays and lesbians. However, lesbians remain doubly discriminated against by the state, as women and as lesbians, and lesbian groups in Spain are currently working on visibility campaigns. At the Coordinadora Lesbiana-Gai Forum in January 1996, one of the topics of discussion was new families.

Legislation

1995 was a good year for lesbians and gays living in Spain. In some towns and cities there is now a register of *de facto* couples. There is no law legislating partnership relations for same-sex couples, but Spain has three laws which recognize benefits for them, all approved under the government of Felipe Gonzalez and the socialist PSOE (Partido Socialista Obrero Espanol).

The law of Urban Arrangements, in which de facto couples are recognized regardless of their sexual orientation, was the first step for full equality for lesbian and gay couples. Legislating the contract for renting a flat or a house, it gives the same rights to married couples, and to de facto couples who can prove that they have been living together for at least two years. In November 1995, a new penal code was approved that penalizes discrimination on the basis of sex, ethnicity, religion and sexual orientation, thereby recognizing the right of sexual orientation as a fundamental human right. And at the end of the year a law on aid and assistance for victims of violent crime and against sexual liberty was passed, which included homosexual couples, specifying that lesbians and gays can be the beneficiaries of aid for spousal injuries.

These three laws served to highlight the lack of a law of *de facto* couples. With this in mind, and the prospect of the imminent general election in 1996, the Coordinadora Gai-Lesbiana launched a campaign, *Vota Rosa* ('Vote Pink'), with the aim of influencing the electoral programmes of the parties.

There is no a specific legislation for homosexual parents. If a lesbian couple have a child together through insemination, only the biological mother has any rights over the child. If the biological mother dies, the child is legally an orphan.

Insemination, adoption and fostering

In Spain, single women have access to insemination. It is not limited to married couples or to heterosexual women. Unmarried couples are

not allowed to adopt or foster children. Single people are allowed to
adopt or foster children, but it is very difficult.

Support groups

Coordinadora Gai-Lesbiana (CGL): operates a free telephone hotline
for the whole of Spain (also from abroad); gives out information on
Spain; lobbies Parliament; advises other lesbian and gay groups; runs
a lesbian group; conducts AIDS–related work; and publishes a magazine, *Pink Barcelona*.

Coordinadora Gai-Lesbiana
c/o les Carolines, 13
08012 Barcelona
Catalunya
Tel: 34-3-237 08 69
Fax: 34-3-218 11 91
hotline: 900 601 601 (from Spain)
34-3-237 70 70 (rest of the world)
e-mail: cogailes@pangea.org
http://www.pangea.org/org/cgl

COGAM-Colectivo de Gais y Lesbianas de Madrid,
Carretas No. 12, 3 pisa 2a puerta,
Apartado de correos 3277-
28080 Madrid
Tel: 91-522-4517
Fax: 91-522-4517

EHGAM in Euskalherria (Basque country)

Sweden

CECILIA BERGGREN
Compiled May 1995

Statistical overview

Source: Bureau of Statistics

Capital: Stockholm

Population: 8.75 million, 4.3 million men and 4.4 million women

Languages: Swedish: although the vast majority of the population speaks Swedish, Finnish is spoken by 4–5% and Lapp by 0.2%.

Ethnic groups: 0.5 million people belong to ethnic minority groups

Religions: Evangelical Lutheran (official) 89%, other Protestant 1.1%, Roman Catholic 1.7%, Russian Orthodox 1.1%, Muslim 0.8%, other 6.3% including 16,000 Jews and 3000 Buddhists.

Marriages: married men and women: 3.3 million

Divorces: divorced men and women: 657,000

Registered same-sex partnerships: approximately 90 partnerships have been registered since the law came into force on 1 January 1995. Seventy-five per cent of these partnerships are between gay men.

Births: 14 per 1000 (1993)

117,998 children were born in 1993

Deaths: 11 per 1000 (1993)

Infant mortality: 5 per 1000 (1992)

Life expectancy: 81.9 for women, 76.2 for men (1994)

General climate and indicators

The situation for gays and lesbians in Sweden has gradually changed for the better since 1944 when homosexuality was still considered a criminal offence. Today a law on registered partnerships has been passed and gays and lesbians are much more considered a natural part of society. However, there is still legal discrimination due to the lack of visibility, especially for lesbians.

The vast majority of Swedes accept homosexuality and homosexuals. An opinion poll carried out in 1993 showed that more than half of the population agreed to gays and lesbians being allowed to marry. Lesbians are perhaps more accepted than gay men, as is the situation in many other countries, but people's positive opinions about lesbianism make lesbians even more invisible. The lack of strong lesbian role models is evident. The 'holy' family of father – mother – child is still a strong institution in the public Swedish mind, and the 'family' as a role model is considered a natural part of 'good society', the way things ought to be. This despite the fact that many children grow up in single–parent families.

On the other hand, single mothers have a strong legal status and are well regarded in the public eye. However, absent fathers and lack of male role models have been much discussed due to rising rates of youth violence.

Gay and lesbian parenthood has been debated from the early 1990s. Only some 12 per cent of the population agree to this, according to an opinion poll. People often use arguments such as 'the children will lack male role models', 'the children will become homosexual as well', 'gays would abuse their children sexually', 'the child would be abused in school.'

Unfortunately the economic crisis and high unemployment has recently created a climate where minority groups tend to be less accepted than before, and that of course includes lesbians and gays.

Legislation

A Swedish lesbian mother has the right to the same benefits as any other Swedish single mother.

The child of a lesbian mother is always deemed to be the result of a

previous heterosexual relationship. A lesbian couple, whether registered partners or simply cohabiting, are not allowed joint custody. The
biological parents have custody. They then decide how the shared parenthood should be arranged. The biological mother automatically gets
custody if the couple is not married when the child is born.

The same-sex partner lacks legal protection as a co-mother.
However, this does not affect the legal protection and benefits of the
child.

A lesbian who decides to have an unknown father for her child may
face problems with the social authorities, as Swedish law states there
must be a known father. The father must either sign the birth certificate or the mother must assist the authorities as far as possible to find
the father. Otherwise the child might be excluded from some social
financial benefits. This does not apply to children resulting from
insemination. A lesbian mother is always considered a single mother,
even if she has a same-sex partner in a registered partnership.

The 'lesbian family' does not exist in the eyes of Swedish law. This,
however, never affects the legal status of the child or any financial benefits within the Swedish system. The lesbian couple is protected by the
law on cohabiting or the law on registered partnership. Simply cohabiting offers poor protection when it comes to inheritance and certain
social benefits. Should they marry, the registered partnership of course
offers more protection. The couple is then guaranteed the same benefits as a married heterosexual couple, with the exception of anything
to do with children.

Insemination, adoption and fostering

Donor insemination is only allowed for married heterosexual couples.
Single heterosexual or lesbian women cannot be inseminated within
the health care system. This is controlled by law. Being inseminated at
home in private is, of course, allowed, but the legal status of the child
can be uncertain.

Lesbian couples are not allowed to adopt children. Only married
heterosexuals can adopt a child together. A married heterosexual can
also adopt the child or children of the other partner. Couples in registered partnerships are not allowed any form of adoption. This is clearly stated in the law on registered partnerships.

A single person aged twenty-five or over may be allowed to adopt a child, but it is uncertain if a single lesbian would be allowed to adopt if she stated her sexual orientation. A cohabiting lesbian couple are not allowed to adopt a child together or the child of one of the partners. If one of the women wished to adopt a child of her own, this is not forbidden. However, a Supreme Court verdict from 1993 denied a man living with another man the right to adopt a child on his own.

A lesbian couple, cohabiting or registered partners, might be allowed to become foster parents. There is no law against it, but it remains very unlikely. There is one Swedish case of a gay male couple becoming foster parents for a gay teenage boy. Fostering gay and lesbian teenagers is therefore accepted by the social authorities, otherwise probably not.

Child and family benefits, childcare

The social and financial benefit system for children is well built in Sweden. There is a common child-support system, one and a half years of paid parental leave when the child is born, temporary child benefit, and so on. Of course all this is available for the lesbian mother and her child. Childcare facilities are widely available and also open for lesbians.

The most difficult situation for an unregistered lesbian couple and their child is the fact that the co-mother lacks legal protection. She has no right to paid parental leave or temporary child benefit. If the lesbian couple registers as partners, the co-mother is allowed to share the parental leave if the biological father does not want his share of it. She is also entitled to temporary child benefit.

If the biological mother dies, the custody of the child can be given to the same-sex partner, cohabiting or registered, if the child has been brought up in a lesbian family. However, the authorities consider the best interest of the child strongly. A lesbian has to prove herself to be a fit mother, more suitable than the other biological parent, to get custody. If she will be able to adopt the child is uncertain.

The future

Homosexual families have been put on the public agenda. The issue is often discussed in public and more gay and lesbian parents come out on national television or in the press.

Psychiatrists and social scientists are also showing an interest in these questions and several studies have already been published. This is somewhat promising for the future even if there is still a long way to go. Several Members of Parliament have also proposed motions to change the law on adoptions and inseminations during 1995.

Having a child together for a gay couple is perhaps not so difficult, but there is lot of red tape to cut through and many laws to consider. The legal situation for gay and lesbian families must be made clearer and the laws of adoption must be changed, at least when it comes to adopting stepchildren. It is true that the child enjoys all of society's benefits, but if the biological mother and father die the legal situation becomes unclear. And that is not in the best interest of the child.

Support groups

Gay parents
PO Box 350 S-101 26 Stockholm
tel: (46) 8 736 02 17
contact person: Greger Eman
Network for gay and lesbian parents

RFSK-Radgivningen
PO Box 450 90 S-104 30 Stockholm
tel: (46) 8 736 02 10
contact person: Ann Colleen
Contact group for older children of gay parents

Lesbian Now!
Kocksgatan 28 S-116 24 Stockholm
tel: (46) 8 641 86 16
Social club for lesbians, based in Stockholm, arranges pubs, parties and other social events for women

Golden Ladies
PO Box 450 90 S-104 30 Stockholm
tel: (46) 8 736 02 12
contact person: Boel Matthis
Contact group for lesbians over forty-five

Kvinnohuset (The Women's House)
Snickarbacken 10 S -111 39 Stockholm
tel: (46) 8 10 76 56
Arranges some activities and discussion groups for lesbians

Kvinnohojden
Storsund 90 S-781 94 Borlange
tel: (46) 243 237 07
A feminist school, which attracts a number of lesbians, sometimes
arranges gatherings for lesbian mothers

Switzerland

RUTH HOWALD

Compiled February 1995

Statistical overview

Source: *CIRCA*

Capital: Berne (Bern)
Population: 7,200,000 (1994)
Main languages: French, German, Italian
Number of speakers: With three official languages in Switzerland many people are bi- or even trilingual. At the time of the 1990 census 63.6% spoke German, 19.2% French, 7.6% Italian and 0.6% Rhaeto-Romansh, others, including Serbo-croat, Spanish, Portuguese, Turkish and English 8.9%
Religions: Roman Catholic 46.1%, Protestant 40%, Muslims 2.2%, Old Catholic 0.3%, Jewish 0.3%, other and non-religious 11.1%
Divorces: 13,000 (1990)
Births: 13 per 1000 (1993)
Deaths: 9 per 1000 (1993)
Life expectancy: 81.7 for women, 75.4 for men (1994)
Infant mortality: 6 per 1,000 (1992)

General climate and indicators

On 10 January 1995, a petition was handed to the Swiss Parliament demanding that lesbians and gays be afforded the same rights as heterosexual couples. A petition is the weakest legal method to put pressure on the Swiss government. Its power depends mainly on the number of signatures collected. As this petition had 85,000 signatures, (more than any other in 1994), and because of concerted lobbying, the petition committee expects the government to act.

Legislation

Currently, a lesbian who already has children from a previous hetero-sexual relationship or marriage enjoys all the rights of a biological mother. In many Cantons she will have no difficulty keeping her children after divorce or separation from their father, even if she is open about being lesbian. However, there are several very conservative Cantons, where she might have to face a more homophobic judge and possibly severe obstacles to keeping the children. Although Swiss law says that being a lesbian or a gay man is not a reason to lose custody of children, a homophobic judge may find other 'reasons' to grant custody to the father.

The real problems, though, centre around co-mothering. Since lesbians are not allowed to get married in Switzerland, there is no means by which a co-mother can be legally related to the biological children of her girlfriend, even if from the beginning those children were raised by both women. If the biological mother is absent or dies, the co-mother is completely dependent on the goodwill of:

- the doctor at the hospital if there are decisions to be taken about the treatment of the child in case of illness or accident
- the teacher at the child's school, if there are decisions to be taken concerning the education of the child
- the judge and the department of welfare, if the biological mother has died and the co-mother wishes to stay with the child.

In addition, the children's right to be taken care of by the adults who raised them is not secure in the present situation: the co-mother has no obligation at all to pay maintenance to the biological mother and children.

Insemination, adoption and fostering

At state level there is no regulation by the law concerning AI, or other medical techniques of reproduction such as in vitro fertilization or surrogate motherhood. At the time of writing, such a law is in preparation.

The legal situation at present is as follows: either the Cantons have their own regulations, or if not, the hospitals themselves regulate access.

A lesbian couple wishing to have a child would be advised to first contact a woman, preferably lesbian, gynaecologist whom they can trust. She should be informed about the regulations in the Canton where the couple lives and will also be able to estimate the costs. This varies depending on the hospital, the gynaecologist, and the number of treatments (most often they will need more than one). Of course, the lesbian couple can choose the Canton they wish to be treated in. Big cities such as Zürich, Bern, Basel or Geneva probably have more generous laws and hospital regulations.

For contacts, more specific information and names of suitable gynaecologists in Zürich, it might be useful to attend a meeting of the group 'Lesbians with children', or to contact the lesbian hotline (see section on support groups).

One of the most difficult issues (besides whether to ask for marriage or some kind of registered partnership) is adoption. There seems to be a gap between lesbians and gay men concerning the importance of adoption. For lesbians, especially, the right to adopt the children of her girlfriend, (so-called 'stepchild adoption') is crucial.

The future

Currently lesbians and gay men are in the process of disscussing parenting issues. A consensus will enable concerted action.

Support groups

'Lesbians with children' (Lesben mit Kindern)
Frauenzentrum
Mattengasse 27 8005
Zürich

Lesbian hotline in Zürich: +1 272 7371

Turkey
LISA A. MULHOLLAND
Compiled April 1996

Statistical overview

Sources: *New Women's Initiatives in Central and Eastern Europe and Turkey.* Task force update December 1995 – January 1996; *UNDP Human Development Report,* 1995

Capital: Ankara
Population: 63,405,526 (1995)
Languages: Turkish, Kurdish, Arabic
Ethnic groups: Turkish 80%, Kurdish 20%
Religions: Islam
Births: 25 per 1000
Deaths: 6 per 1000
Infant mortality: 46 per 1000
Life expectancy: 74 for women, 69 for men
Households headed by women: 10%

General climate and indicators

In the 1980s various social and political groups began to organize and agitate for change. Both homosexual and feminist organizations were among these groups and now in the 1990s are beginning to gain both limited respect and responsiblity. At the same time a move towards radical Islam and the growth of a police state make life difficult and sometimes dangerous for writers, intellectuals and journalists.

Working in such a challenging environment, feminist groups have made advances in such areas as publicizing high rates of violence within families as well as obtaining rights for women to control their own wage earning abilities.

Regardless of the gains brought about by feminism, women in Turkey face the challenge of living in a highly patriarchal society where responsiblity to family is a strong social force. Over 60 per cent of women do unpaid work in family businesses, especially in rural areas. The trend is a movement into paid labour, however, with women as about 30 per cent of renumerated workers, mostly in femi-nized industries like the service sector, textiles and teaching, but only 14 per cent hold management positions.

Lesbians have only recently come under public scrutiny and are slowly organizing their own groups and activities. One example are the newly established Sisters of Venus who publish newsletters and flyers as well as give public interviews and speeches. The Turkish feminist monthly *Pazartesi*, a four-year-old publication with a circula-tion of 5,000, covered some of the difficulties of lesbian life in an issue published in late 1995. Three women were interviewed and spoke of both the problems and fears around keeping sexuality hidden from neighbours and family.

Support groups

Pazartesi
Sehit Muhtar Caddesi
60/5 Talimhane Taksim
Istanbul, Turkey

Sisters of Venus
Venüs 'ün
Kizkardesleri, MBE 165
Kayisdag Cad. no: 99
Ziverbey, Istanbul

United Kingdom

CATHERINE DONOVAN

Compiled May 1995

Statistical overview

Sources: Central Statistical Office, (1994) *Annual Abstract of Statistics*, G. Dennis (ed.) (London: HMSO); Central Statistical Office (1994) *Social Trends*, J. Church, (ed.) (London: HMSO); Central Statistical Office (1993) *Key Data 1993/94*, G. Dennis, (ed.) (London: HMSO); Thomas, M., Goddard, E., Hickman M., and Hunter, P. (1994) *General Household Survey 1992* Series GHS No. 23 London: HMSO)

Capital: London
Population: 57,000,000
Ethnic groups: English predominantly. Indian 1.5%, Black (Carribean, African and other) 1.6%, Bangladeshi, Pakistani, Chinese, Arabic
Religions: Church of England, Roman Catholic minority also Muslim, Sikh, Hindu, Jewish, Mormon, Jehovah's Witness, Spiritualists
Marriages: 12 per 1000 (1991)
Divorces: 13 per 1000 (1991)
Births: 13.2 per 1000
Deaths: 13.5 per 1000
Infant mortality: 7.4 per 1000 live births
Mothers: 7,000,000
Single mothers/households headed by women: 1,300,000 (1991)

General climate and indicators

The late 1980s and 1990s have seen the advent of a lesbian baby boom (*Pink Paper*, 1989). Many more lesbians than ever before have chosen or are choosing to parent, and a perusal of the personal columns of the lesbian and gay press indicates some of the methods by which lesbians and gay men are making mutually beneficial arrangements. Nevertheless the social and political climate in which lesbians are choosing parenthood is a mixed one. At a public level, party political and Government statements and policy decisions reflect a hostile response, which simultaneously idealizes one type of family – traditional, heterosexual, married, nuclear family, while penalizing all other types – especially those headed by single women. The Conservative Government headed by John Major launched a Back to Basics Campaign that attempted to encourage 'traditional' family values. This came hot on the heels of the Thatcher government's crusade against lesbians and gay men, and single and cohabiting heterosexual couples.

Since the mid-1980s, several pieces of legislation have been enacted which seek to reward, sustain and encourage married, heterosexual nuclear family life, while punishing, disenfranchising and discouraging any other forms. Single mothers have been particularly singled out as the cause of family and societal breakdown: they have shouldered the blame for delinquency, drug use and the housing crisis. Several Conservative MPs have suggested that pregnant single women might be 'encouraged' to give their babies up for adoption by the married heterosexual couples who cannot have their own children (*Pink Paper*, 1993). Even Tony Blair, the Leader of the opposition Labour Party, stated that he thought it better for children to be brought up in a family with two parents. Both legislation and prevailing attitudes are saturated with heterosexist values, which have created a society where lesbian mothers can be in fear for their children, themselves, their homes, and their way of life.

At the same time there has been an unprecedented amount of media coverage that has not been all negative (Studzinksi, 1994). Three out of four mainstream UK soap operas now feature central lesbian characters and storylines; the media is full of lesbian chic imagery; and BBC and Channel 4 television channels proposed new lesbian and gay television series for late 1995, one of which will be aimed at specifically at a lesbian audience (*Pink Paper* 1995). Meanwhile lesbian mothers in the UK carry on bringing up their children alone, with partners or with close friends and family, and some achieve personal victories which validate their families and their status as mothers. In early 1994, for example there was media coverage of a lesbian couple who successfully used the Children Act 1990 to establish parental rights based on co-residence with their children. There is also the feeling that custody cases, once the burning issue for lesbian mothers in the 1970s and early 1980s, are now much more winnable and likely to be settled by decisions based on the welfare of the child rather than on the mother's sexuality (Dilly, 1990; Marchbank, 1991). However, there are still some judges who cannot get past the mother's sexuality and act on their prejudices both against lesbians and in favour of heterosexual couples (e.g. *Pink Paper*, 1988).

In the autumn of 1994, two incidents occurred that graphically illustrated how difficult is the struggle to establish rights for lesbian mothers. First came the Save the Children Executive decision to rescind an invitation to Sandy Toksvig to host their annual event. Ms Toksvig, a stand-up comedian and television personality, had just come out in a Sunday newspaper article in which she talked about her life with her partner and their children. The furore that ensued (including pressure from high-level employees within the organization) forced the charity to apologize to Ms Toksvig but it came too late for her to fulfil her engagement. The second blow came when the Children's Society passed a policy decision to reject all lesbians and gay men as potential adoptive parents. The campaign to bring about change is still in progress.

Legislation

In the UK, same-sex relationships have no legal validity and lesbian couples are not allowed to register as such either in a civil or mainstream religious ceremony. The Metropolitan Community Church and some Unitarian congregations perform rites of blessings of relationships in which rings or tokens may be exchanged, but these ceremonies have no legal standing.

The Local Government Act 1988, Section 2(a) (better known as Section 28) makes it illegal for local authorities to intentionally promote homosexuality, or for children in schools to be taught that lesbian and gay families are anything other than 'pretend' family relationships (Colwin and Hawksley, 1991). Although the Act does not affect sex education, as school sex education policies are determined by school governors, nevertheless it has created an atmosphere in which homophobic councils or councils fearful of legal challenge have made decisions, that have resulted in a denial of the validity of lesbian and gay life, including lesbian parenting (Studzinski, 1994).

The Child Support Act 1991 came into force in April 1993 and set up the Child Support Agency to replace the way in which maintenance orders were made through the courts for the children of women who were separated from the children's father. Any single parent can apply to the Agency for maintenance. However, for those single women in receipt of certain state benefits (Income Support, Family Credit and Disability Working Allowance) they must either name the father, or give an acceptable reason why they cannot do so. The penalty is the loss of 20 per cent of their personal allowance for six months and 10 per cent for a further twelve months.

The Children Act 1989 is the only piece of legislation that enables lesbians to protect their status as co-parents. In 1994 two women with a 22 month-old-son were awarded a joint residence order giving the mother's partner equal parental responsibility as long as they share a residence (Williams, 1994). The Children Act allows any 'significant adult' in a child's life to apply for a residence order. The official solicitor confirmed that two other lesbian couples have used the Act in this way (Williams, 1994).

Insemination, adoption and fostering

In 1990 the Human Fertilisation and Embryology Act (HFEA) made it a legal responsibility for licensed clinics to take into account the welfare of children who would be born as a result of any treatment services, 'including a child's need for a father' (HFEA, 1990: Para 2, clause 5:14). This was introduced largely because of right-wing fears that lesbians and single heterosexual women were using donor insemination to have children without men. The Act also made it illegal for any third parties, other than those in licensed clinics, to handle donated gametes. This means that any informal SI networks in which people act as go-betweens to provide anonymous sperm could be in breach of the Act. Both this Act and the Children Act 1989 carry the presumption that children need fathers (Rights of Women, 1992). Men who donate sperm through licenced clinics sign away any parental rights and obligations so that children born are legally fatherless. However, men who donate through SI would still be considered in the same way as an unmarried father, regardless of his actual involvement with any children. Under the guidelines to the Child Support Act 1991, donors are liable for maintenance for any children born as a result of their sperm donations in SI arrangements (Rodgerson, 1993). This could have several effects for lesbian mothers: potential donors might be reluctant to donate sperm, so making it more difficult for lesbians to achieve parenthood; some donors who are forced to make maintenance payments might decide to ignore any prior arrangements made and demand previously unwanted participation in the lives of children for whom they are providing money; donors or previous husbands or partners might want to establish parental responsibility for children for whom they are being forced to pay maintenance.

In 1990 in Newcastle upon Tyne, the local newspaper caused an outcry when it reported a lesbian couple had had a disabled child placed with them. Eventually the child was removed from their care and placed with his previous foster carer, who had wanted to adopt him herself but had not been offered the opportunity. The furore that arose as a result of the case had national implications. In December of that year, the Department of Health produced guidelines for the Children Act in which Paragraph 16 stated that 'No-one has a "right" to be a foster parent. "Equal rights" and "gay rights" have no place in the fostering services.' (Woods, 1991). A campaign led by lesbians and gay men and which included many organizations like the Children's Society, the National Society for the Prevention of Cruelty to Children (NSPCC), Barnardos and Save the Children UK was successful in having the wording removed.

In 1992 a Department of Health discussion paper, 'The Adoption Process' invited views on a range of adoption issues including lesbian and gay adoption (*Capital Gay*, 1992). In 1993, the government's white paper on adoption was written without any reference to the exclusion of lesbians and gay men as adoptive parents (*Capital Gay*, 1993) although the Minister for Health made a statement that 'It is not possible for homosexual couples to adopt now and we don't intend it to be possible for homosexuals to adopt' (*Gay Times*, 1993, p. 8).

However, she did say that lesbians and gay men as single people might be considered in the same way as other unmarried hetero-sexuals.

In reality local authorities make their own policies about whether lesbians and gay men will be considered for adoption and fostering. In 1991, the Conservative-controlled Brent Council in London passed a policy specifically barring lesbians and gay men from being considered as foster parents (Saxton, 1991). After a three-year battle, two women in Hampshire, a county in the South of England, were accepted by their County Council Social Services Committee as foster parents (Rodgerson, 1993). In Sunderland, a city in the North of England, a lesbian was allowed to foster her two nephews, but a Conservative spokesperson condemned the decision saying that 'I'm not homophobic, but I would like to see these children fostered by a normal family – perhaps where there are other children' (*Pink Paper*, 1988). The Council defended its decision on the grounds that lesbians and gay men have the right to foster and adopt and it was common practice to appoint a relative to care for children.

Child and family benefits, childcare

Currently, parents who are claiming Income Support because they are unwaged qualify for a Family Premium or a One-Parent Premium and receive an additional payment for each child. All parents (regardless of circumstance) are entitled to claim Child Benefit which is £10.80 per week for the first child, and approximately £8 for subsequent children. Single parents can claim One Parent Benefit which is £6.30 per week. With all state benefits, levels are reduced if couples are living together especially if there are two biological mothers living together, each of whom qualifies for the full amount.

Childcare provision is particularly poor compared with the rest of European Union. There is no compulsory schooling until age five, and although most schools offer some pre-school nursery education this varies enormously: in some areas it is only for one term before school age, in others all three- and four-year-olds can get a nursery place. There are a whole range of private day nurseries and pre-school play groups which are fee-paying. Most local authorities offer a limited number of day nursery places to children, usually prioritizing those who are deemed to be in particular need. Most children of working parents are cared for by a child minder or nanny, either registered with the local authority or in a private arrangement with relatives or friends.

The future

The ideological strength of the heterosexual nuclear family is formidable and reflected in the rhetoric and social and economic policies of the government, other political parties and in some sections of the voluntary sector. However, the reality is that this family form is just one type among many types that co-exist in the UK in the 1990s. The future is to be found in recognizing and giving equal status to these diverse living arrangements. That movement has already begun in the lesbian and gay community. More and more books are being written and research is being conducted to discover and analyse the diversity of family relationships in which lesbians and gay men are involved – including the different ways in which lesbians achieve parenthood and live as lesbian mothers.

A number of important issues need to be debated and discussed by lesbian mothers, co-parents and other lesbians and gay men involved in the lives of children. How to cope with complex arrangements which are new and possess no role models. How to create ways of dealing with relationship breakdowns and donors and parents who change their minds about the extent of their involvement. How we ensure that not only those who identify as co-parents but also those who are significant adults in children's lives are recognized and validated not just by the 'outside' world of officialdom, schools, doctors and families of origin but within our lesbian and gay communities, networks and families.

For many lesbian mothers, especially those who are black and/or poor, the future looks grim. The struggle must continue at two levels: to change heterosexist government policies which discriminate against single women who head households. Second, to create within lesbian and gay child-friendly spaces and trust and support for lesbian mothers, many of whom are fighting for their right to exist.

Support groups

Many local lesbian mothers groups are established, develop and then cease to exist, making it difficult to compile an up-to-date list of local groups. However, they often advertise in the *Pink Paper*, the UK's only national lesbian and gay newspaper, or they can be found by phoning the local Lesbian Line, Lesbian and Gay Switchboard or Lesbian Custody Project (see below).

Lesbian and Gay Fostering and Adoption Network
c/o London Friend
86 Caledonian Road
London N1 9DN
tel: 0171 837 2782 (women only)

Lesbian Custody Project, Rights of Women
52 Featherstone St
London EC1Y 8RT
Advice and support for lesbians involved in mothering or wanting to mother, in relation to the law.

Lesbian Line is located in almost every part of the UK. To find out the nearest one to you phone London Lesbian Line 0171 253 0924 Mon and Fri 2 p.m. – 10 p.m. and Tues and Thurs 7 p.m. – 10 p.m.

London Lesbian and Gay Switchboard can put you in touch with your nearest Switchboard or Lesbian Line. tel: 0171 837 7324. 24-hour service.

Positive Parenting
PO Box 7
1 Newton Street
Manchester M1
Mixed campaigning group working towards equal rights in adoption and fostering for lesbians and gay men.

SHAKTI (South Asian Lesbian, Gay and Bisexual Helpline)
c/o London Friend
Tel: 0171 278 7806 or 01850 120 274

Bibliography

Ali, Turan (1996) *We Are Family: Testimonies of Lesbian and Gay Parents*, London: Cassell.

Anderson, Shelley (1995) *Lesbian Rights Are Human Rights*, Amstedam: ILIS.

Arnup, Katherine (ed.) (1995) *Lesbian Parentship: Living with Pride and Prejudice*, Charlottetown, Canada: Gynergy Books.

Barclay Mandel, Jane and Hotvedt, Mary E. (1993) Lesbians as parents: a preliminary comparison of heterosexual and homosexual mothers and their children, *Luisarts & praktijk* 4.

Benkov, Laura (1994) *Reinventing the Family: Lesbian and Gay Parents*, New York: Crown.

Bourne S. (1995) Shocks on the box, *Pink Paper*, 376, April, p.15.

Bowen, Angela (1990) *Children In Our Lives: Another View of Lesbians Choosing Children*, Brookline: Profile Productions.

Capital Gay (1992) Should gays adopt? 530, February.

Capital Gay (1993) No change on adoption policy, 624, December.

Chan, Sucheng (1993) You're short besides!, in Margaret L. Anderson and Patricia Hill (eds) *Race, Class and Gender: An Anthology*, New York: Wadsworth.

Clunis, D. Merilee and Green, G. Dorsey (1995) *The Lesbian Parenting Book: A Guide to Creating Families and Raising children*, Seattle: Seal Press.

Colwin, M; and Hawksley, J. (1989) *Section 28: A Practical Guide to the Law and its Implications*, London: National Council for Civil Liberties.

Corrin, Chris (ed.) (1992) *Superwomen and the Double Burden*, London: Scarlet Press.

Dennis, G. (ed.) (1993) *Key Data 1993/94*, London: HMSO.

Dennis, G. (ed.) (1994) *Annual Abstract of Statistics*, London: HMSO.

Dilly, A. (1990) Beyond the fight for custody, *Pink Paper*, 106, January, p. 12.

Dineen, Claire and Crawford, Jackie (1990) Lebiantics, *Fireweed* 28.

Dodds, Dinah and Allen-Thompson, Pam (1994) *The Wall in my Backyard: East German Women in Transition*, Boston: University of Massachusetts Press.

Gibbs, D. (1989) Lesbianism: offering non-traditional roles, *Women and Therapy* 8, pp.1–2.

Gilligan, Carol, Lyons, Nora P. and Hanmer, Trudy J. (eds) (1990) *Making Connections: The Relational Worlds of Adolescent Girls at Emma Willard School*, Cambridge, MA: Harvard University Press.

Green, Richard, Barclay Mandel, Jane, Hotved, Mary E., Gray, James and Smith, Laurel (1986) Lesbian mothers and their children: a comparison with solo parents, hetrosexual mothers and their children, *Archives of Sexual Behaviour* 15 (2).

Hanscombe, Gillian E. and Forster, Jackie (1982) *Rocking the Cradle: Lesbian Mothers A Challenge in Family Living*, London: Sheba.

Hoeffer, Beverly (1981) Children's acquisition of sex-role behavior in lesbian mother families, *American Journal of Orthopsychiatry*, 51.

Human Fertilisation and Embryology Act (1990) London: HMSO.

ILGA (1993) *Conference Report: Eastern and South Eastern Europe*, Vienna: HOSI.

ILIS (International Lesbian Information Service*) Newsletter* Issues 1994–96

Kirkpatrick, Martha (1992) Middle age and the lesbian experience, in Margaret L. Anderson and Patricia Hill (eds) *Race, Class and Gender: An Anthology*, New York: Wadsworth.

Lewin, Ellen (1993) *Lesbian Mothers: Accounts of Gender*, Ithaca: Cornell University Press.

Marchbank, J. (1991) Lesbian motherhood, *Gay Scotland*, 55, February, p. 9.

Martin, April (1993) *The Guide to Lesbian Parenting*, London: Pandora.

Miller, Jane (1994) State, family and personal responsiblity: the changing balance for lone mothers in the United Kingdom, *Feminist Reveiw* 48, Autumn, pp. 24–69.

Miller, Judith Ann, Brooke Jacobson, R. and Bigner, Jerry J. (1994) The child's environment for lesbian vs. heterosexual mothers: a neglected area of research, *Journal of Homosexuality* 7(1), pp. 49–55.

NGO Forum (1995) *The Gender Gap in Eastern Europe and the CIS: Impact of Transition*, Beijing: NGO Forum.

Oleker, Eileen and Walsh, Linda U. (1984) Childbearing among lesbians: are we meeting their needs? *Journal of Nurse-Midwifery* 29 (5), September/October.

Pagelow, Mildred D. (1980) Heterosexual and lesbian single mothers: a comparison of problems, coping and solutions, *Journal of Homosexuality* 5(3), Spring.

Parikas, Udo and Ueispak, Teet (eds) (1991) *Sexual Minorities and Society*, Talinn, Estonia: Institute of History.

Patterson, Charlotte J. (1992) Children of lesbian and gay parents, *Child Development* 63.

Pies, Cheri (1985) *Considering Parenthood: A Workbook for Lesbians*, San Francisco: Spinsters/Aunt Lute.

Pink Paper, (1988) Row breaks out over lesbian fostering, 317, March 4.

Pink Paper (1993) Tories launch attack on single mothers, 299, October p. 1.

Pollack, Sandra and Vaughn, Jeanne (eds.) (1987) *Politics of the Heart: A Lesbian Parenting Anthology*, New York: Firebrand Books.

Pranluv Issues from 1995 and 1996.

Rand, Catherine, Graham, Dee L. R. and Rawlings, Edna, I. (1982) Psychological health and factors the court seeks to control in lesbian mother custody trials, *Journal of Homosexuality* 8(1), Autumn.

Reinhold, Susan (1994) Through the parliamentary looking glass: 'real' and 'pretend' families in contemporary British politics, *Feminist Review* 48, Autumn, pp. 61–79.

Rights of Women (1986) *The Lesbian Mothers Legal Handbook*, London: Women's Press.

Rights of Women (1992) Self-insemination and the new laws: a Rights of Women Lesbian Custody Group briefing paper. Prepared for the Lesbian Motherhood and the New Laws Conference, March 1992.

Robson, Ruthann (1992) Mother: the legal domestication of lesbian exis- tance, *Hypatia* 7(4), Autumn.

Rodgerson, G. (1993) Ordinary people, *Gay Times*, 177, June, p.16

Saffron, Lisa (1994) *Challenging Conceptions: Planning a Family by Self- Insemination*, London: Cassell.

Saffron, Lisa (1996) *What about the Children? Sons and Daughters of Lesbian and Gay Parents Talk about their Lives*, London: Cassell.

Saxton, A. (1991) Tories shut door on adoption, *Capital Gay*, August, p. 9.

Shawstack Sassoon, Anne (1987) *Women and the State*, London: Routledge.

Streib, Uli (ed.) (1996) *Das lebisch-schwule Babybuch*, Berlin: Quereverlag GmbH.

Studzinski, K (1994) *Lesbians Talk Left Politics*, London: Scarlet Press.

Task Force Update: Newsletter of the Lesbian and Gay Immigration Rights Task Force, December 1995–January 1996, New York.

Thomas, M., Goddard, E., Hickman, M. and Hunter, P. (1994) *General Household Survey 1992*, London: HMSO.

UNDP (1995) *Human Development Report*, New York: Oxford University Press.

Walker, Lisa M. (1993) How to recognize a lesbian: the cultural politics of looking like what you are, *Signs*, Summer.

Weston, Kath (1993) Parenting in the age of Aids, in Stein, Arlene (ed.), *Sisters, Sexperts, Queers: Beyond the Lesbian Nation*, London: Plume.

Williams, F. (1994) Lesbian couple granted parental rights, *Gay Times*, 191, August, p. 29.

Woods, C. (1991) Government will revise fostering guidelines, *Gay Times*, March, p. 16.